THEY HAVE LEFT US HERE TO DIE

DELETED

GLENN ROBINS

They Have Left Us Here to Die

The Civil War Prison Diary

of Sgt. Lyle Adair,

111th U.S. Colored

Infantry

The Kent State
University Press
Kent, Ohio

© 2011 by The Kent State University Press, Kent, Ohio 44242

ALL RIGHTS RESERVED
Library of Congress Catalog Card Number 2011016812
ISBN 978-1-60635-101-7
Manufactured in the United States of America

Lyle G. Adair's diary is reproduced courtesy of
Andersonville National Historic Site.

Library of Congress Cataloging-in-Publication Data
Adair, Lyle, b. 1843.
They have left us here to die : the Civil War prison diary of Sgt. Lyle Adair, 111th U.S.
Colored Infantry / [edited and annotated by] Glenn Robins.
p. cm. — (Civil War in the North)
Includes bibliographical references and index.
ISBN 978-1-60635-101-7 (hardcover : alk. paper) ∞
1. Adair, Lyle, b. 1843—Diaries.
2. Prisoners of war—Confederate States of America—Diaries.
3. Prisoners of war—United States—Diaries.
4. United States—History—Civil War, 1861–1865—Prisoners and prisons.
5. Military prisons—Confederate States of America—History.
6. Captivity narratives—Confederate States of America.
7. United States—History—Civil War, 1861–1865—Personal narratives.
8. United States. Army. Colored Infantry Regiment, 111th (1864–1866)
9. United States—History—Civil War, 1861–1865—Regimental histories.
I. Robins, Glenn.
II. Title.
E611.A33 2011
973.7'13—dc23
2011016812

British Library Cataloging-in-Publication data are available.
15 14 13 12 11   5 4 3 2 1

CONTENTS

Preface

LYLE G. ADAIR, LIKE SO MANY Civil War soldiers, was a largely unknown figure. A few details about the onetime sergeant of Company B of the 111th United States Colored Infantry can be derived from the fragmentary evidence of the federal census records and his military personnel records. An exception to the lack of primary source material is Adair's self-titled diary "Seven Months in Prison," which recounts in vivid detail his experiences as a prisoner of war in the Confederate prison camps of the Deep South.[1] There is a certain degree of symmetry here regarding the number seven. Approximately, one out of every seven soldiers of the American Civil War became a prisoner of war, and, of that number, one out of every seven "perished at the hands of their captors." Adair's story is in many ways a very unique and personal narrative, yet his experience also speaks for thousands of anonymous comrades who were left to die in the human dungeons known as Civil War prisons.[2]

There were a combined 409,608 prisoners of war; the North held 214,865 and the South held 194,743.[3] The *Official Records of the War*

---

1. Lyle G. Adair Diary, ANDE accession number 484, ANDE catalog number 3686, Andersonville National Historic Site, Andersonville, Georgia (hereafter ANHS).

2. A total of 56,194 prisoners died in captivity, 30,218 Union soldiers and 25,976 Confederate soldiers. Charles W. Sanders Jr., *While in the Hands of the Enemy: Military Prisons of the Civil War* (Baton Rouge: Louisiana State Univ. Press, 2005), 1.

3. Ibid.

of the Rebellion identifies thirty-two "principal places for the confinement of Union prisoners held by Confederate authorities." Of that number, thirteen camps were located in the Deep South states of Georgia and Alabama.[4] From September 1864 to April 1865, Sgt. Lyle Adair was held in five of these prisons: Cahaba, Millen, Blackshear, Thomasville, and Andersonville. In many of these camps, Union war prisoners encountered great hardships as they faced incarceration without adequate food, clothing, shelter, or medical treatment. Those who survived held to the possibility of being paroled or exchanged. But for most, including Sergeant Adair, that dream only came to fruition after months of captivity and toward the literal end of the war.

A relatively small number of Civil War prisoners published accounts of their captivity experience. Although twenty-six accounts appeared in 1865 and 1866, "production slowed in the 1870s," and while former prisoners continued to offer their stories to the reading public, the yearly average of the decade of the 1880s and 1890s was less than two published accounts per year. A variety of motives inspired the former prisoners to construct written records of their plights. Some were driven by a desire to "document the patriotism of captured soldiers," others hoped to bear witness to deliberate mistreatment at the hands of brutal captors, and many sought to establish "testimony" necessary for securing a government pension.[5] Despite the very real instances of suffering in captivity, the postwar recollections often contained "exaggerations and misrepresentations."[6] One former prisoner, Jesse Hawes, seemed intent on provid-

4. The Georgia camps were Americus, Andersonville (Camp Sumter), Atlanta, Augusta, Blackshear, Millen (Camp Lawton), Macon (Camp Oglethorpe), Marietta, and Savannah. The Alabama camps were Cahaba, Mobile, Montgomery, and Tuscaloosa. U.S. War Department, *War of the Rebellion: A Compilation of the Official Records of the Union and Confederate Armies,* 128 vols. (Washington D.C.: GPO, 1880–1901), ser. II, vol. 8:1004 (hereafter *OR*).
5. Ann Fabian, *The Unvarnished Truth: Personal Narratives in Nineteenth-Century America* (Berkeley: Univ. of California Press, 2000), 121, 226.
6. William Marvel, "Johnny Ransome's Imagination," *Civil War History* 41 (Sept.

ing a ranking of comparative suffering: "When the facts are known Cahaba must go down in history as worse in a great many respects than Andersonville or any other military prison of the Confederacy."[7] Because of the legitimate concerns over the credibility of postwar narratives, the Adair diary offers a less distorted and more reliable interpretation of the prisoner-of-war experience.

This book is not a biography of Lyle Adair. The primary purpose of *They Have Left Us Here to Die* was to transcribe Adair's diary, add contextual annotations, and provide an analytical paradigm for interpreting the Civil War prisoner-of-war experience. In Chapter 1, I tried to reconstruct Adair's military service prior to capture with special attention to the controversial decision to enlist black troops and the experience of white soldiers who served with those freedom fighters. Chapters 2 through 6 are the edited diary itself. Wherever possible, footnoted annotations were used to either explain certain issues or situations or to compare Adair's observations with his fellow prisoners or, in a few instances, with those of his captors. Furthermore, in order to understand the prisoner-of-war experience, one must also know the history of the prison camps as well as their surrounding communities. At the beginning of these chapters, a headnote is provided to help the reader place Adair's captivity experience within the broader context of Confederate prisons as well as the Southern home front. The final chapter, Chapter 7, offers a systematic framework for reading prisoner-of-war accounts. By utilizing the seven captivity narrative event scenarios—precapture, capture, removal, landscape, resistance, release, and lament—the reader can avoid a fixation on such mundane matters as descriptions of the weather and rations and focus on the essential themes of the prisoner experience.[8]

1995): 188. See also William B. Hesseltine, "The Propaganda Literature of Confederate Prisons, *Journal of Southern History* 1 (Feb. 1935): 56–66.

7. Jesse Hawes, *Cahaba: A Story of Captive Boys in Blue* (New York: Burr, 1888), 461.

8. Robert C. Doyle, *Voices from Captivity: Interpreting the American POW Narrative* (Lawrence: Univ. Press of Kansas, 1994), 85.

In most instances, I have reproduced the diary's original formatting. At the start of the diary, Adair employed a narrative style, and not until November 4, 1864, did he begin the process of the more traditional daily diary entries. Therefore, I provided artificial breaks for ease of reading. I also inserted the chapter divisions and chapter titles, but all other headings were written by Adair. Aside from some necessary punctuation, I have made no corrections to the text of the diary. Rather than riddle the diary with the corrective [*sic*], I preserved the misspellings of such words and places as forrest, Johnston Island, Fort Sumpter, and, most notably, Henry Wirtz. I have also omitted three poems that Adair composed after his release, in January and February of 1867: "Dedicated to a Friend on Their 18th Birthday," "The Old Bachelors Life," and "Musings at Sea."

Acknowledgments

I AM INDEBTED TO MANY for the completion of this book, but, perhaps above all, I am indebted to place. I live a mere fourteen miles from the Andersonville National Historic Site (ANHS). Most do not realize that the ANHS, a component of the National Park Service, is not only the site of the Civil War's most infamous prison, but it is also the site of an active national cemetery and the National Prisoner of War Museum. To live in southwest Georgia, one must actually strive to ignore the story of America's prisoners of war. As a Virginian, I am unable to ignore place.

Alan Marsh, cultural resources specialist at the ANHS, first alerted me to the existence of the Lyle G. Adair diary. He also helped me select the images for the book. Mark Stibitz, an extremely knowledgeable and long-serving volunteer at the ANHS, shared his own research on Adair, which included Adair's military service and pension records.

At the Kent State University Press, I received enthusiastic support and valuable commentary from Lesley J. Gordon, the Civil War in the North series editor. The anonymous reader for the Press provided a thorough and detailed assessment of the first draft and offered several key suggestions that helped transform the manuscript into a book. Acquiring editor Joyce Harrison also made this project a very pleasant task.

At Georgia Southwestern State University, Gary Fisk helped me prepare the images for submission. Colleagues Richard Hall, Brian Parkinson, and Ellen Cotter survived numerous stories and updates about the diary project. I also received institutional support from the university in the form of faculty development grants.

My graduate school friend Thomas Ward took time away from his own busy research agenda to read and comment on the first draft of the manuscript, and his wise words resulted in major changes in the conceptualization of the project. My parents, Marvin and Phyllis, have always given me unconditional love and support. And Kim Douglas—although she read and critiqued the entire manuscript—my debts to her are more numerous, and ones that can never be repaid.

CHAPTER 1

The Unknown Soldier

LYLE ADAIR WAS BORN to Benjamin and Nancy Templin Adair on April 11, 1843, in Vigo County, Indiana. Sometime prior to 1860, Adair moved to Boone County, which had been organized by the State of Indiana in 1830 from territory that "had been acquired from the Indians by the Federal government in a treaty made at St. Mary's, Ohio, in 1818." There Adair lived in Sugar Creek Township, in the northwest corner of the county. Its "rich and undulating" lands and "the remarkable fertility of the soil in this flat district" produced bountiful crop yields. "One of the most beautiful stretches of water in the Hoosier state," Sugar Creek coursed through the county. The rural midwestern community possessed sawmills, carding mills, steam flouring mills as well as a variety of churches, among them Methodist Episcopal and Presbyterian. There was also a small group of Quakers in the township's Sugar Plains community.[1]

The 1860 federal census listed Adair as a resident of the Lyons House Hotel. James S. Adair, presumably a relative, was the hotel's landlord. The thirty-five-year-old James and his wife and young children lived in the hotel with twelve other tenants, a group that included several carpenters, a miller, a saddler, several merchants, and even a professor of music. Lyle Adair and one other resident

---

1. *History of Boone County, Indiana* (Lebanon, Ind.: Boone County Historical Society, 1984), 6, 45; L. M. Crist, *History of Boone County Indiana* (Indianapolis, Ind.: A. W. Bowen, 1914), 97.

1

reported farming as their occupation. Although little is known about Adair as a farmer, one friend, Arden P. Middleton, who "was well acquainted" with Adair and "lived on an adjacent farm," described him as "an able bodied young man," and James Wilson considered Adair to be of "steady habits and good moral character."[2]

The Indiana teenager began his military career on August 30, 1861, when he enlisted as a sergeant in Company C of the 81st Ohio Volunteer Infantry (OVI). No doubt, the financial incentive of the bounty system enticed a large number of young men to answer the call to arms during the early stages of the war. In the North, Congress passed a law in May 1861 that permitted the federal government to offer a bounty, or payment, to military volunteers "of up to $300." State and local governments could also contribute to the "bounty pool." Recruitment was a pressing issue throughout the summer of 1861 with President Abraham Lincoln receiving congressional approval to enlist as many as 500,000 volunteers.[3] Perhaps monetary rewards offered during the summer rush to expand the Union military tempted Adair, who apparently had not achieved any type of meaningful material success. And the young bachelor had lost his father in March 1854 and did not seem to have any binding familial obligations. Yet, Adair's diary contains numerous references to his love of country and expressions of unwavering patriotism. These values clearly played an essential role in sustaining him during his seven months in captivity and may have been his motivation for enlisting.

The 81st Ohio formed at Greenfield under the command of Capt. Robert N. Adams. According to regimental historian Maj. W. H. Chamberlin, the 81st Ohio was "an organization, which, perhaps, is

2. A photocopy of the census data appears in the Lyle Adair Folder (hereafter LAF), M653, roll 245, p. 884, provided by Mark Stibitz. A notation in pen indicates that the copy was from the 1860 federal census of Boone County. The Middleton and Wilson comments appear on affidavits used by Adair to apply for a prisoner-of-war pension. Photocopies of the affidavits appear in LAF.

3. David S. Heidler and Jeanne T. Heidler, *Encyclopedia of the American Civil War: A Political, Social, and Military History*, 5 vols. (Santa Barbara, Calif.: ABC-CLIO, 2000), 1:256–57.

unlike that of any other regiment sent into the field from Ohio. It is an adopted child of the State, not one of the manor born." In August 1861, the 20th Ohio was mustered out after having fulfilled its initial three-month commitment. The unit was not reconstituted, "as was the case with most of the other three months' regiments of Ohio." However, several officers of the 20th Ohio determined to form an "independent regiment, without the aid of the State," and intended to muster "singly, or in squads, or companies" with Gen. John C. Fremont, whose headquarters were in St. Louis, Missouri.[4] The group adopted the name Morton's Independent Rifle Regiment, but "by some bad management . . . one full company . . . was actually taken possession of by Col. Crafts J. Wright, of Cincinnati, who was also organizing an independent regiment." Additional companies were in danger of being siphoned off. As a result, "State pride fortunately intervened" and the 81st Ohio was commissioned by the authority of the governor of Ohio and its legislative members.[5]

During the winter months of 1861–62, Adair's Company C and the 81st Ohio spent a great deal of time in northern Missouri as part of the Department of Missouri. Their mission involved "scouting, arresting accomplices and principals in the work of destroying the railroad, and in restoring peace and quiet to the whole country round about."[6] Chamberlin recalled nothing exceptional about these military tasks, nor did Corp. Charles Wright, a member of Adair's Company C. February of 1862 was, however, an interesting time in the military life of Lyle Adair as he was "reduced to the ranks" on the fifth day of the month. Unfortunately, Adair's service records do not provide an explanation for his demotion to private.[7]

4. W. H. Chamberlin, *History of the Eighty-First Regiment Ohio Infantry Volunteers: During the War of the Rebellion* (Cincinnati, Ohio: Gazette Steam, 1865), 9.

5. Charles Wright, *A Corporal's Story: Experiences in the Ranks of Company C, 81st Ohio Vol. Infantry During the War for the Maintenance of the Union, 1861–1864* (Philadelphia: John Beale, 1887), 10–11.

6. Chamberlin, *History of the Eighty-First*, 14.

7. A photocopy of Adair's military service records appears in LAF.

The lack of excitement in military activities was offset by "a thrilling episode" that occurred after the 81st Ohio took possession of Fulton, Missouri, in early 1862. "We heard a voice in our rear," Corporal Wright recalled, "and a moment later a young colored boy about eighteen years old dashed into our ranks exclaiming, Save me boys! Save me! Old Master is after me, and he will kill me!" The slaveholder and one associate brazenly entered the Union lines and demanded the return of his runaway slave. The slave had embedded himself with the ranks of Company C, which forced the slaveholder to approach the company's captain for assistance. Capt. Robert N. Adams refused to comply. Then one of the officers of Company C delivered a "sword-stroke" that sent the mounted slaveholder "into the bushes." Still undeterred, the slaveholder made one final appeal to a superior officer, Lt. Col. John A. Turley. Despite the slave's plea for protection, and the "click, click, of a dozen muskets," Turley, who claimed he lacked the authority to offer safe haven to the fugitive, ordered the would-be-contraband back to his owner. According to Wright, after Turley departed, several members of his company approached the slaveholder and informed him, "We're going into camp not far from here, will be around here for some time, and if we ever hear tell of your abusing this boy we'll come and burn every d--d thing you've got!" On another occasion during a camp "grumble" concerning inadequate rations and chilly weather, Wright advised a comrade, "Maybe you had better go over and join the fellows on the other side and become satisfied." After a moment of reflection, the grumbler replied, "When you write to your friends in Oxford tell them that I am just as black an abolitionist as you are."[8]

The men of the 81st Ohio could have developed their antislavery views prior to their enlistment. Ohio produced notable abolitionists, such as Levi Coffin and John Rankin, and the Buckeye State served as a major route on the Underground Railroad. Ohio was also the scene of one of the nation's most publicized runaway slave rescue cases. In

8. Wright, *A Corporal's Story*, 15–16, 22.

the Oberlin-Wellington rescue case, state and federal officials and courts clashed over the legal interpretation of the Fugitive Slave Act of 1850. One rally in Cleveland drew more than 10,000 people, and some demonstrations resulted in mob violence.[9] Another possible explanation was that the men of the 81st Ohio had been influenced by the Fremont Proclamation. Gen. John C. Fremont, the first Republican presidential candidate, commanded the Union's Western Department during the summer of 1861 and oversaw operations in the hotly contested border state of Missouri. From late July to late September, Fremont "lost nearly half of Missouri." Facing logistical problems, supply and troop shortages, and "the increasing boldness of guerrillas," Fremont made a bold decision. On August 30 the political general "placed Missouri under martial law, proclaimed the death penalty for guerrillas captured behind Union lines, and confiscated the property and freed the slaves of all Confederate sympathizers." For his actions, Fremont received praise from abolitionists and a significant number of Republicans. President Abraham Lincoln, however, fearing defections among slaveholding Unionists in all border states, ordered Fremont to amend the proclamation to conform with the First Confiscation Act passed by Congress on August 6, 1861. This legislation allowed for the seizure of "slaves, used in the military aid of the rebellion." As historian James McPherson has explained, the First Confiscation Act "applied to only a handful of slaves then within reach of Union forces, and it did not specifically emancipate them." Fremont's declaration greatly exceeded the army's legislative authority as defined by the First Confiscation Act, and when Fremont ignored Lincoln's demand, the president relieved the controversial general of his command.[10]

9. For a convenient summary of these aspects of Ohio's antislavery history, see "Oberlin-Wellington Rescue Case," *Ohio History Central*, July 1, 2005, http://www. ohiohistorycentral.org/entry.php?rec=522; and "Underground Railroad," ibid., http:// www.ohiohistorycentral.org/entry.php?rec=1518. Each article contains references and suggested readings.

10. James McPherson, *Ordeal by Fire: The Civil War and Reconstruction* (New York: Knopf, 1982), 156–58, 267.

The anecdotes from the regimental histories of the 81st Ohio seem to confirm the findings of historian Chandra Manning, who maintains that slavery occupied a central position in "the Union soldiers' understanding of the war." According to Manning, the "commitment to emancipation was created by and during the war itself." The development of emancipationist views evolved as Northern soldiers encountered slaves and Southern society for the first time. These interactions convinced many Union soldiers that slavery was a national, not exclusively Southern, sin, one that they, by force of arms, could "erase and atone" for. The Fremont Proclamation resonated and inspired those who had come to accept this sacred mission of national cleansing. Emancipation, however, did not guarantee equality, and as Manning suggests, "white Union troops strove to separate slavery from the more complicated issues of black rights and racial equality, embracing abolition while evading hard questions about what the nation owed the former slaves."[11] Manning's work challenges earlier studies by such historians as James McPherson and Reid Mitchell, who examined the ideological and cultural convictions of Civil War soldiers and determined that, for the majority of Northern fighters, the abolition of slavery was not a primary war aim. "While restoration of the Union was the main goal for which they fought," McPherson contends, "they became convinced that this goal was unattainable without striking against slavery." Moreover, "the attitudes of a good many soldiers on this matter were more pragmatic than altruistic." Similarly, Mitchell argues that "hatred of slaveholders did not necessarily imply love for the slave." In fact, "most Union soldiers . . . did not support emancipation."[12] Based on the relatively few instances in which Adair mentioned race in his diary, one would have to assume that the Hoosier was not a doctrinaire abolitionist.

11. Chandra Manning, *What This Cruel War Was Over: Soldiers, Slavery, and the Civil War* (New York: Knopf, 2007), 12–14, 46–47, 219.
12. James McPherson, *For Cause and Comrades: Why Men Fought in the Civil War* (New York: Oxford Univ. Press, 1997), 118–19; Reid Mitchell, *Civil War Soldiers* (1988; repr., New York: Penguin, 1997), 14. For ethnic-based studies of the abolition

In March 1862, the 81st Ohio moved to St. Louis and was assigned to the Second Brigade, Second Division of the Army of the Tennessee. This new assignment placed the unit on the front lines of some key battles in the Western Theater for most of 1862. At Shiloh, generally viewed as the first major battle of the war where many raw volunteers saw the elephant for the first time,[13] the 81st Ohio played an important role in stabilizing the federal lines after the initial Confederate attack. Late on the morning of April 6, the first day of the battle, the 81st was part of a mile-and-a-half-long "makeshift perimeter" established at Pittsburg Landing after the collapse of the Union right flank. Repositioned for the afternoon, the 81st participated in "one of the final delaying actions on the Federal left" at Cloud Field. The next day the 81st advanced as part of the federal counterattack that eventually forced the Confederate Army to withdraw from the field of battle.[14] The first man of Company C to fall on the battlefield at Shiloh was none other than Capt. Robert Adams, who on the first day "was struck in the head by a grape-shot and died instantly."[15]

In the realm of what-if history, Shiloh could be viewed as the Confederacy's best opportunity for military success in the Western Theater and could have possibly altered the outcome of the war. But the certainty of the Union victory abetted the federal thrust into the crucial Mississippi Valley. In the fall of 1862, the 81st Ohio helped repel the Confederate offensive against the Union-held town of Corinth, Mississippi. On both October 3 and 4, the 81st defended a position around Battery Powell, one of two points of concentration

issue, see Martin W. Oefele, *German-American Speaking Officers in the U.S. Colored Troops, 1863–1867* (Gainesville: Univ. Press of Florida, 2004), 3; and Susannah U. Bruce, *The Harp and the Eagle: Irish-American Volunteers and the Union Army, 1861–1865* (New York: New York Univ. Press, 2006), 121, 133–34, 150–51. Neither Oefele nor Bruce finds much support among German and Irish Americans for abolition or the Emancipation Proclamation.

13. Joseph Allan Frank and George A. Reaves, *"Seeing the Elephant": Raw Recruits at the Battle of Shiloh* (New York: Greenwood Press, 1989).

14. Larry J. Daniel, *Shiloh: The Battle That Changed the Civil War* (New York: Simon & Schuster, 1997), 245, 225.

15. Wright, *A Corporal's Story*, 36.

that largely determined the outcome of the battle in favor of the Union.[16] The regiment lost eleven men; forty-four were wounded, and three were listed as missing. Among those numbers, Adair's Company C had no deaths, six wounded, and one missing, Amos Swartz "never since heard from."[17] This Union victory prevented a Confederate advance into West Tennessee and ended any possibility of a concerted Southern effort in the liberation of Kentucky.[18]

The 81st Ohio wintered at Pulaski, Tennessee. "The winter of 1863–4 was a severe one," Corporal Wright recalled. "The citizens of Pulaski stated that it was the coldest they had known for many years, consequently picket-duty was severe around the encampments."[19] There were a few minor cases of frostbite but "no serious ones." Warmth may have been in short supply, but the subject of reenlisting radiated throughout the regiment. The War Department had recently issued orders regarding the reorganization of veteran forces. Specifically, "troops who had less than a year to serve under their existing enlistment, and who had served at least two years, could, by re-enlisting for three years or during the war, unless sooner discharged, obtain a discharge from their present enlistment, get the bounty of one hundred dollars which was to be paid at the end of the their three years' service, have a furlough of thirty days immediately upon re-enlisting, and get a veteran bounty in installments amounting in all to $402." Companies B, C, D, E, and F of the 81st Ohio were eligible for this reenlistment program. Maj. W. H. Chamberlin admitted that all did not reenlist, but he was proud and confident that "the majority of the young men re-enlisted."[20] In fact, roughly seven out of ten members of Company C reenlisted, remained on

16. Peter Cozzens, *The Darkest Days of the War: The Battles for Iuka and Corinth* (Chapel Hill: Univ. of North Carolina Press), 196–97, 242.

17. Chamberlin, *History of Eighty-First*, 32–33.

18. For an overview of the strategic significance of Shiloh and Corinth, see Steven E. Woodworth, *Jefferson Davis and His Generals: The Failure of Command in the West* (Lawrence: Univ. Press of Kansas, 1990), 86–109, 125–62.

19. Wright, *A Corporal's Story*, 81.

20. Chamberlin, *History of the Eighty-First*, 71, 73.

detached service, or transferred to other units and served beyond their original three-year enlistments.[21]

Among those who accepted the army's offer for reassignment was Pvt. Lyle Adair. He enlisted with the 3rd Alabama Colored Infantry, later renamed the 111th U.S. Colored Infantry (USCI). In his diary, Adair did not reveal the factors that led him to make this fateful decision. Historian Joseph Glatthaar identifies several possible explanations for why white individuals joined the colored troops. Some "felt sympathy for the black race and wanted to help elevate them through service, while others saw this as an opportunity to aid the cause of the Union more than they could through service in white volunteer units." Also, serving with black units "provided many soldiers with an opportunity to increase their salary and obtain a command position that simply was unattainable in their volunteer unit."[22] Personal advancement certainly appealed to Ohioan Samuel Evans, who left the 70th OVI, where he held the rank of private, to join the 59th United States Colored Troop (USCT) at the rank of lieutenant. In explaining his decision to his disapproving father, Evans argued, "My place is easier than a privates, have better quarters and more privileges." But Evans also believed "that a Negro is no better than a white man and has just as good a right to fight for his freedom and the government."[23] In his case, Adair did receive a promotion, serving as a noncommissioned officer at the rank of sergeant, a position he initially held with the 81st Ohio and a reasonable appointment given the need for experienced soldiers in the black units.

Whatever motivated Adair, he made a choice that would have profound consequences. Indeed, Glatthaar contends, "as officers in

21. This information is based on a review of Ohio Roster Commission, *Official Roster of the Soldiers of the State of Ohio in the War of the Rebellion, 1861–1866,* 12 vols. (Akron, Ohio: Werner, 1886–1895), 6:478–82.

22. Joseph Glatthaar, *Forged in Battle: The Civil War Alliance of Black Soldiers and White Officers* (New York: Free Press, 1990), 39.

23. Robert F. Engs and Corey M. Brooks, *Their Patriotic Duty: The Civil War Letters of the Evans Family of Brown County, Ohio* (New York: Fordham Univ. Press, 2007), 155–56.

the USCT, they were at times pariahs in their own army, ridiculed by some white volunteers and separated from their enlisted men by racial, cultural, and military barriers under the enormous stress of military service in the USCT, and amid their sense of isolation . . . for years and years afterward they bore its emotional scars, and seldom did they receive care or even compassion for their injuries." Because of these considerations, it is not surprising that only three of the roughly seventy-five eligible members of Company C joined Adair in accepting an assignment with a black unit. All four men would serve in the 111th USCI and at a rank higher than what they held with the 81st Ohio. In addition to Adair, the list included Sgt. William H. Scroggs, who was promoted to captain and ended the war as a lieutenant colonel; Sgt. John Mader, who served as quartermaster sergeant; and Cpl. Joseph K. Nelson, who was promoted to first lieutenant and regimental quartermaster.[24]

Sometime during May or June of 1863, Adair accepted a "detached service" assignment. Under orders from Gen. Grenville M. Dodge, Adair served as a recruiting agent for the 3rd Alabama. Adair then spent the summer of 1863 recruiting for the 2nd Alabama, but there were no notations in his service records for the months of September and October or for November and December. In late January 1864, Adair accepted his discharge from the 81st Ohio in order to be promoted to sergeant with the 3rd Alabama.[25] As a recruiter, Adair would have likely visited any number of contraband camps in the states of Alabama, Tennessee, and Mississippi. The term "contraband" became part of the military's lexicon early in the war as Union commanders addressed the legal status of slaves who entered their lines with the intention of preventing their return to their masters. Viewed as the "contraband of war," the former slaves would now fight to liberate those still remaining in bondage.[26] Of

24. Glatthaar, *Forged in Battle*, 242; *Official Roster of the Soldiers of the State of Ohio*, 6:478–82.

25. A photocopy of Adair's military service records appear in LAF.

26. Kate Masur, "'A Rare Phenomenon of Philological Vegetation': The Word 'Contraband' and the Meanings of Emancipation in the United States," *Journal of American History* 93 (Mar. 2007): 1050–85.

the more than 93,000 black soldiers from the seceded states of the Confederacy, the three states of Alabama, Tennessee, and Mississippi provided 42,971 soldiers, slightly less than half the total.[27]

When Adair left for his recruiting assignment, contraband camps had already become an established component of the Union war effort in the Western Theater. The contraband camp at Corinth, Mississippi, epitomized the military's infrequent success in dealing with the freedmen and became "a birthplace of freedom for thousands of blacks." Indeed, as historian Cam Walker has written, "for more than a year, from late 1862 to early 1864, the contraband camp at Corinth provided the first taste of non-slave life for men, women, and children who had fled the plantations of Mississippi, Tennessee, and Alabama." This site of a pivotal battle in October 1862 served as a refuge for 1,500 to 6,000 slaves. In military terms, men such as Gen. Grenville Dodge, commander of the Corinth District, and Gen. Ulysses S. Grant viewed the contraband camps as a way of protecting "the health and morale" of their men from the disruptive effects thousands of fleeing slaves would cause to the logistical operations of their units. Grant in particular was intent on advancing on Vicksburg and refused to be burdened by the black evacuees. Moreover, contraband camps provided laborers to "various departments of the army."[28]

This process began by first organizing the freedmen into a productive group of agricultural workers, which usually meant "picking, ginning, and baling the cotton crop already standing in the southern fields" as well as the cultivation of vegetable gardens that were sufficiently large to feed the camp population. In addition, the former slaves participated in formal education and religious education programs, many of which were coordinated by the American Missionary Society. "As the contrabands also maintained their own blacksmiths, shoemakers, carpenters, and seamstresses, purchased all of their clothing, and paid a poll tax of a dollar a month," Cam

27. Bell Wiley, *Southern Negroes, 1861–1865* (New York: Rinehart, 1938), 311.

28. Cam Walker, "Corinth: The Story of a Contraband Camp," *Civil War History* 20 (Mar. 1974): 5–8.

Walker concludes, "Corinth had in late spring of 1863 become . . . [a] kind of independent community" replete with houses, streets, schools, hospitals, and a commissary. Early in 1863, President Lincoln indirectly added a new military dimension to the Corinth Contraband Camp when the Emancipation Proclamation authorized the use of black soldiers in the Union Army. Prior to official War Department authorization, the camp commandant, Chaplain James M. Alexander of the 66th Illinois Volunteers, "created a company of black soldiers" who were drilled and supervised by two white soldiers. Ultimately, Commandant Alexander formed an entire black regiment, the 1st Alabama Infantry of African Descent, later to be renamed the 55th USCI. The 1st Alabama guarded the camp and a series of outposts "until January 1864, when the garrison and the freedmen were transferred to Memphis."[29]

Transforming contraband into soldiers and building a biracial regiment was a difficult task. At the very least, white soldiers and former slaves had to minimize the cultural differences that existed between them, and many white soldiers had to deal effectively with any preconceived ideas of black inferiority. In many instances, noncommissioned officers were selected through a process of trial and error. As Glatthaar notes, "In one month the 65th United States Colored Infantry reduced thirty-two noncommissioned officers to the ranks and filled their slots with new men."[30] Adair appeared to have avoided such purges, or possibly benefited from them, and maintained his rank as sergeant during his service with the 111th USCI. Whatever personal difficulties Adair may have encountered, some signs of unit success appeared on June 25, 1864, when the men from the 3rd Alabama Colored Infantry officially formed the 111th USCI.

Stationed in Pulaski, Tennessee, the regiment served in the District of North Alabama, Department of the Cumberland, and was tasked with guarding rail lines between Pulaski and Athens, Alabama.

29. Ibid., 7–17.
30. Glatthaar, *Forged in Battle,* 102–3; Brian Steel Willis, *A Battle from the Start: The Life of Nathan Bedford Forrest* (New York: HarperCollins, 1992), 251–54.

When given the opportunity, black soldiers acquitted themselves well in direct combat, but most were assigned to "garrison or fatigue [labor-related] duty," such as that performed by the 111th USCI. Although less likely to be killed in action, black units suffered a death rate by disease that "was almost twice as high" (19 percent) as that of Northern white soldiers. Therefore, these rear-guard areas, where medical supplies, surgeons, and doctors were in short supply, were not without substantial risks.[31] In September 1864, Adair and the men of the 111th USCI faced an equally threatening enemy, the South's most famed cavalryman, Gen. Nathan Bedford Forrest.

31. McPherson, *Ordeal by Fire*, 354.

CHAPTER 2

Capture

BETWEEN SEPTEMBER AND October 1864, Gen. Nathan Bedford Forrest waged an impressive campaign against Union railroad positions in northern Alabama and middle Tennessee. The slave-trading Mississippian had been called into action by the newly appointed commander of the Confederate Department of Alabama, Mississippi, and East Louisiana, Gen. Richard Taylor, son of former Mexican War hero and U.S. president Zachary Taylor. Forrest's objective was to disrupt Union supply routes along the Memphis & Charleston Railroad and the Nashville & Decatur Railroad. For some time Confederate authorities had been considering cavalry raids as a way of impeding Gen. William T. Sherman's assault on Georgia. Although they eventually made a decision to attack Union supply lines, they had waited too long to prevent the fall of Atlanta. Sherman captured the city on September 2. At that time, the Confederates were uncertain of Sherman's next move. His Atlanta position afforded him several options, including some combination of moves against the Alabama cities of Montgomery or Selma. Sherman's other option, which he ultimately selected, was a strike through central and eastern Georgia. Within this context, Taylor advised Forrest to provide some type of "relief" to Gen. John Bell Hood's Army of Tennessee, which was then situated west of Atlanta. Success most likely involved the disruption of Sherman's communications lines

Of the Civil War prison camps identified on this map, Adair spent time at Cahaba (2), Camp Lawton (6), and Camp Sumter (8). Courtesy of Andersonville National Historic Site.

1. Bell Isle, Richmond, Virginia
2. Cahaba Prison, Cahaba, Alabama
3. Camp Chase, Columbus, Ohio
4. Camp Douglas, Chicago, Illinois
5. Camp Florence, Florence, South Carolina
6. Camp Lawton, Millen, Georgia
7. Camp Morton, Indianapolis, Indiana
8. Camp Sumter, Andersonville, Georgia
9. Castle Pickney, Charleston, South Carolina
10. Elmira Prison, Elmira, New York
11. Johnson's Island, Sandusky, Ohio
12. Libby Prison, Richmond, Virginia
13. Old Capitol Prison, Washington, D.C.
14. Point Lookout, Point Lookout, Maryland
15. Rock Island, Rock Island, Illinois
16. Salisbury, Salisbury, North Carolina

"north of the Tennessee River." Therefore, Forrest needed to "move his cavalry in that direction at the earliest moment."[1]

By mid-September, Forrest had arrived at Cherokee Station, a small rail town on the Memphis & Charleston line in northwestern Alabama. He immediately began making preparations for the upcoming campaign. In addition to the roughly 3,500 men Forrest brought with him from Mississippi, he also had under his command the forces of Generals P. D. Roddey and Joseph Wheeler. The combined force totaled approximately 4,500 raiders, although some operated independently of Forrest's direct command. There were two primary strikes during the September–October campaign of 1864. The first took place at and around Athens, Alabama, the only major federal fortification on the Nashville & Decatur Railroad and a community that had previously experienced some of the most intense and racially charged military operations of the war.[2] On September 23, Forrest forced the surrender of the 110th USCI and several companies of the 111th USCI. Just two days later, the Mississippi cavalryman moved on to Sulpher Springs, where he met Col. William H. Lathrop and the remainder of the 111th, including Sgt. Lyle G. Adair.[3]

1. Quote from Richard Taylor, *Destruction and Reconstruction: Personal Experiences of the Late War* (1879; repr., Nashville: J. S. Sanders, 1998), 203; Robert Dunnavant Jr., *The Railroad War: N. B. Forrest's 1864 Raid through Northern Alabama and Middle Tennessee* (Athens, Ala.: Pea Ridge Press, 1994), 1–12.

2. Dunnavant, *The Railroad War*, 25–35; Willis, *A Battle from the Start*, 251–52; Roy Morris Jr., "The Sack of Athens," *Civil War Times Illustrated* 24 (Feb. 1986): 26–32; George C. Bradley and Richard L. Dahlen, *From Conciliation to Conquest: The Sack of Athens and the Court-Martial of Colonel John B. Turchin* (Tuscaloosa: Univ. of Alabama Press, 2006).

3. Willis, *A Battle from the Start*, 251–54.

Lyle G. Adair
August 1st 1865

Seven Months in Prison
By 1st Sergh L. G. Adair of 111th U.S. Colored Inf

Our Capture

[September 24] On the evening of the 23rd of September, 1864, the garrison of Sulphur Fosstte Ala. was startled by the hard pearls of artillery in the direction of Athens, distant eight miles. Various were the surmises, as to what the cause of it was, by the little garrison commanded by Col. [William H.] Lathrop, and composed of five companies of the 111th U.S. Colored Infantry namely Co's A, B, H, I, J. Early the next morning the sounds increased for awhile, then died away. In the evening the news came that Athens had been taken by the Rebel Genl. Forrest and he was marching in the direction of Sulphur [Branch] Trestle. Initially every thing was excitement and bustle in preparing to meet the foe. We were reinforced by one battalion of the 3rd Tenn Calvary and two companies of the 9th Ind Cavalry amounting in all to some six hundred effective men. The evening and night was slowly away and still no sign of our being attacked.

[September 25] Just at seven in the morning of the 25th, the pickets commenced firing, soon one could distinguish the rebel lines advancing. Then the artillery opened and the fighting became general on every side. About eleven o'clock Col. Lathrop was killed: a braver man, or truer officer never breathed the air of heaven than he. About one o'clock Forrest sent in a demand for the surrender of the fort. After holding a council of war we were surrendered by Col. [J. B.] Minnis of the 3rd Tenn Cavalry for we were out of ammunition & could not defend ourselves longer against such overpowering numbers, Forrest having some 15,000 men & we only some 600. We were immediately marched out of the fort and started in the direction of the Tenn River.

[September 26–28] On the 26th marched hard all day. My wound, which I received was much inflamed and troubled me very much; could not have got along had not Lieut. [Harry D.] Workman gave me his horse to ride, which I rode most of the day; crossed the Tenn River at Bainbridge Ferry, seven miles above Florence, and marched to Tuscumbia on the Memphis and Charleston Railroad reaching there on the morning of the 28th of Sept.

[September 28–29] There we got the first we had to eat since our capture except a little corn we begged from our guards when they were feeding their horses. Here we drew flour and a little fresh beef. Had no way of cooking the flour so we mixed it with water and poured it around sticks, and stuck them in the ground before the fire and thus baked by turning the sticks when one side was baked. Lay here until the morning of the 29th when we marched to Cherokee Station, distant 15 miles. At Cherokee found the prisoners captured at Athens. Col. [J. A.] Dewey took the news of Lathrop's death very hard.[4] He was on detached duty at Athens, and was captured the day previous to us and knew nothing of our fate until we were brought in to Cherokee.

[September 30] On the 30th all the officers left for Meridian. They came down and bid us good bye. Sad indeed was the parting. I could not help but weep at the sad and sudden death of our brave Col. But more sad was our having to part with our officers.[5] But they were gone and we were left here awaiting our removal to some Southern dungeon, perhaps to spend the remainder of our existence.

4. Colonel Dewey had been with Col. Wallace Campbell, 110th USCI, at Athens, Alabama, on September 24, the day before Lathrop's death, and was already a prisoner as a result of Campbell's controversial surrender. *OR,* ser. I, vol. 39:499. For more on the Campbell surrender, see chapter 7 herein.

5. In most cases, North and South, officers were not confined in the same areas as enlisted men; officers were usually held in separate camps. The primary officer camps in the South were Libby and Danville (Virginia) and in the North Fort Warren and Johnson's Island (Ohio). Officers were also held in separate areas within the

[October 5]

Leaving Cherokee Station, October 5th 1864

Lay here six days, it was raining most of the time. We had no covering but the canopy of the heavens about and no bed but the earth
beneath to lay upon. Still we were happy in the thought that our
sufferings were for our country, and for the defense of the union and
universal freedom. This evening the cars came, and we got on board
cattle cars the stench of which was almost suffocating, went as far as
Iuka, Miss. where we lay over night. One of my comrades and I had
planned our escape had they traveled after night. But their stopping
before dark prevented our putting our plans into execution.

[October 6–7] We were quartered in the upper story of a large building, and were not allowed to go down stairs. Early next morning
were put on board of the train and started for Corinth when near
Glendale the train ran off the track causing quite a smash up. I was
standing looking out of the car door at the time of the accident, and
all at once found myself lying full length in the far end of the car
considerably stunned by the suddenness of the accident. We then
had to get off the train and march nine miles to Corinth reaching
there by one o'clock p.m. At night were put in the building which
was formerly used as post commissary when the Union troops were
stationed here.

[October 8–10]

Making a Rebel Acquaintance

I got acquainted with Hank Brown an orderly sergeant of the 15th
Tenn, who seemed to be a very fine man. ~~considering a rebel can be
a fine man.~~ He took us out to the hotel where our provost marshal's

---

same camp. According to historian Lonnie Speer, the rationale "for separating the two
classes was most likely out of the belief that officers, because of rank, were entitled
to, or deserved, better quarters, increased privileges, and preferential treatment over
that of the enlisted men." Lonnie Speer, *Portals to Hell: Military Prisons of the Civil
War* (Mechanicsburg, Pa.: Stackpole Books, 1997), 58–59.

offices used to be to get our breakfast. Had a very good meal for the South. Paid three dollars apiece in Confederate money for a meal. They took us out twice a day to get water like so many cattle. Remained here until the morning of the 9th of Oct. when we took the train for Meridian, Miss. Nothing of any importance occurred, and at sun down we reached West Point, where we lay over night. This is a beautiful place and nicely situated. I could not help noticing the seaming hatred of soldiers in active service for those at home, guarding the rail roads and stations. One instance that came under my observation occurred at Gainesville Junction where one of the new issue soldiers was standing upon the platform when the cars came up and stopped. What! said he to one of the guards, did you take these white men and the niggers fighting together. The guard replied in the affirmative, when he remarked that *he* would never take a white man and a nigger alive who were fighting together. Yes, said the guard you are very careful to never go where there is any chance to take them, and accused him of being a cowardly house guard afraid of going to the front, but could talk and abuse unarmed Yankees when they were brought down there where he was in no danger. Early next morning we started on for Meridian and reached there by 4 o'clock p.m. where we were put in the stockade for the night. H[enry] Thomas of my regiment here.

CHAPTER 3

Cahaba

ON OCTOBER 11, 1864, LYLE ADAIR arrived at the sleepy little town of Cahaba, Alabama, the site of one of the Civil War's most fascinating prison facilities. The town seat of Dallas County, once the former state capital, rested at the confluence of the Cahaba and Alabama rivers some ten miles south of Selma. It was equidistant between Demopolis, forty miles to its west, and Montgomery, forty miles to its east. Surrounded by navigable rivers and railroad lines, the town prospered somewhat during the late 1840s and early 1850s as a shipping hub for cotton and corn. However, the interlude of economic success ceased by 1860. Population figures were one indicator of the town's declining fortunes and evidence that residents were looking elsewhere for opportunities for personal betterment. Between 1850 and 1860, the total population (white and slave) fell by almost 50 percent to roughly 2,700.[1] When the Civil War broke out, Cahabans fell victim to *rage militaire*, a patriotic fever that engulfed the entire county. "Political meetings were a nightly occurrence," according to one resident, and "many of the most prominent and wealthy men" enlisted in the army, equipped companies of soldiers, or "made generous contributions to the government in money and negroes to work on the breastworks at Selma and Mobile." As the

---

1. William O. Bryant, *Cahaba Prison and the* Sultana *Disaster* (Tuscaloosa: Univ. of Alabama Press, 1990), 1, 29, 74; Bert Neville, *A Glance at Old Cahawba, Alabama's Early Capital* (Selma, Ala.: Selma Printing Service, 1976), 1–8.

war progressed, those who remained in Cahaba found life increasingly difficult. Adjustment and adaptation were the by-products of a community that lacked most essential commodities. Sometimes items were available, but prices were exorbitant, and most citizens simply did without the basic goods that were so readily available before the war. Although the people of Cahaba experienced their share of hardships, the town and county were spared of any destruction wrought by the Union Army.[2]

Cahabans did directly encounter the Union Army on a daily basis for an extended period of time when the Confederate government decided to locate a prison camp in the heart of their town. The exact date of the prison's origin is unknown, and at some point the prison also became known as Castle Morgan, mysteriously named after the famed Confederate cavalryman John Hunt Morgan. One historian places the establishment of the prison in the "spring or summer of 1863." Originally, the Alabama site served as a collection station for Union prisoners who were being dispersed to various detention centers throughout the South. It evolved from this temporary status into a permanent facility. Apparently, Cahaba ceased to function as an actual prison for a brief period when the Confederacy opened a camp at Andersonville, Georgia. All of Cahaba's prisoners, except for those who were too sick to travel, were transferred to Andersonville in mid- to late May 1864. However, when the Andersonville population grew to unmanageable heights, Cahaba officially reopened in late June 1864 and remained open for the remainder of the war.[3] Adair's confinement at Cahaba lasted from October 11 to October 29, 1864. Historians have estimated that Cahaba held as many as 5,000 prisoners during its existence. The prison had a capacity of 500, but

2. "Life in Dallas County During the War," *Confederate Veteran* 24 (May 1916): 216–22. There were two military units raised in Dallas County. The most highly regarded of the two was the Cahaba Rifles, Company F, 5th Alabama Infantry, which operated with the Army of Northern Virginia. The other unit, Lewis's Cavalry Battalion, was organized later, on January 21, 1863, and was assigned to Col. Charles G. Armistead's 12th Mississippi Cavalry Brigade and operated in Alabama and Georgia.

3. Bryant, *Cahaba Prison and the* Sultana *Disaster,* 23–24.

the maximum number of prisoners held at any one time was 3,000, which was the population figure when the prison finally closed.[4]

During the final four months of the war, which Sergeant Adair spent at Andersonville, the Union prisoners of war at Cahaba experienced two extraordinary events. The first began on the afternoon of March 1, when the banks of the Cahaba and Alabama rivers began to overflow. Within a few hours, water covered the grounds of the prison stockade. Contemporary accounts of the camp flood place the depth of the water in the compound between eighteen inches and four feet. Prisoners, of course, sought relief and requested a transfer to higher ground. Prison officials denied the request, fearing that prisoners would attempt to escape during a transfer. Little was done to ease the plight of the prisoners during the first three days of the flood. They were left to their own devices and received a once-a-day ration of crackers. Although approximately 700 prisoners were finally transferred to nearby Selma, the roughly 2,300 who remained were forced to survive in the mud and debris for an additional ten days or so until the water receded.[5]

The second, more tragic, event occurred at the end of the war. News that the war had ended brought hope to Cahaba's captives, and prisoners from throughout the South converged on Vicksburg, Mississippi, where they eagerly anticipated their return to freedom. On the evening of April 24, 1865, nearly 2,300 civilian passengers and former prisoners boarded the USS *Sultana*. The exact number on board has never been determined because the muster rolls were not completed prior to departure. However, sources agree that the *Sultana* passenger total exceeded the ship's certified limit by five to six times. The overcrowding was just one problem. On arriving at Vicksburg, the ship's engineer discovered that the vessel's boilers were leaking badly. After repairs were made, the *Sultana* reached Memphis on the evening of April 26. After a brief stop, the

4. Speer, *Portals to Hell,* 332.
5. Bryant, *Cahaba Prison and the* Sultana *Disaster,* 108–11; Hawkes, *Cahaba: A Story of Captive Boys in Blue,* 448; Speer, *Portals to Hell,* 259.

ship continued northward. Then, around 2 A.M. one of the boilers exploded, toppling the smokestack and causing massive structural damage to the ship. Some former prisoners died instantly in the explosion. Those who survived the initial blast were forced to jump overboard. Already weak and in poor health from their incarceration, the former prisoners now faced a final desperate struggle that many were unable to overcome. Approximately 800 survivors were rescued, but more than 1,500 former prisoners either drowned or died in the wreckage of the *Sultana*. In a note of bitter irony, most of the country paid little attention to the *Sultana* tragedy, because less than two weeks earlier John Wilkes Booth had shot and killed President Abraham Lincoln and the nation was still mourning the loss of the Great Emancipator.[6]

[October 11, 1864] Early on the morning of the 11th we were put on board the train and started on our [illegible] for Selma, Alabama. Reached McDonald on the Tombigbee River when were just on board the boat *Magones*[?] and went four miles up the river to Demopolis where we again took the train for Selma reaching there by 4 o'clock p.m. We were then marched down to a wood yard where we staid all night. Selma is a beautiful place, furnishes more large guns and ammunitions of war than any other city in the Confederacy at this time. After remaining overnight we were marched through the city down to a wharf where we were put on board the packet *Gentirrds*[?], and started down the Alabama River to Cahaba, distant 20 miles by the River. Reached there by 1 o'clock p.m. Here we were searched and put in prison.[7]

6. Bryant, *Cahaba and the* Sultana *Disaster*, 115–18.

7. On arrival at Cahaba, prisoners were searched and "their money, watches, and other valuables" seized. They received credit for these items and could subsequently place orders with a camp purchasing clerk, who was authorized to fill the requests based on account balances. As part of the credit process, prisoners exchanged their Northern currency, or "greenbacks," for Confederate currency at a ratio of one dollar to one dollar. According to one Confederate assistant adjutant and inspector general, "a considerable amount of U.S. currency has thus been accumulated in the hands of camp officials," but the "disposition" of these funds could not be determined. *OR*, ser II, vol. 7:999.

[October 11, cont'd.] The prison is guarded very closely.[8] It is a large brick building formerly a cotton warehouse, enclosed by a large plank fence with sentinels on the outside of the fences, and stationed inside are sentinels with instructions to shoot anyone who may cross or attempt to cross this line, called a deadline.[9] Inside the building there is again another line six feet inside the walls, with sentinels inside the lines with the same instructions.[10]

[October 11, cont'd.] The men were only allowed to go out in the yard and do their cooking. There was some 2,000 men in this building[11] and when all were standing up it was almost impossible to walk around, they were so much crowded.[12] Here they gave us

8. Confederate officials did not agree with Adair's assessment of prison security. One prison investigator deemed the guard force "totally inadequate for the duties required of them" and predicted that the prisoners "need only a little determination and a leader to enable them at any time to over power the feeble garrison . . . [and] easily effect their escape." The guard force consisted of "161 men and 18 detailed men, and two small pieces [of] field artillery." Observers noted that they were "badly armed and their discipline and instruction are very inferior." The detail was also overworked "owing to the small number, they are on duty every other day." Ibid., 1000. The attempted mutiny on January 20, 1865, seemed to confirm the inadequate security at Cahaba.

9. Deadlines were used in both Northern and Southern prisons and were a common feature of stockade-type prisons. In practical terms, the deadline served as a security measure to prevent prisoners from rushing the guards or sabotaging the prison walls in a possible escape attempt. Speer, *Portals to Hell,* 263–64.

10. On March 31, 1864, five months before Sgt. Lyle Adair arrived, R. H. Whitfield, a Confederate prison surgeon, completed the first official report on the facility. He described the major structure at the prison, an unfinished cotton warehouse, as "a brickwall inclosing an area of 15,000 square feet covered by a leaking roof with 1,600 feet of open space in its center, four open windows and the earth for the floor." *OR,* ser. II, vol. 6:1124.

11. By mid-October 1864, the prison population reached a total of 2,151 inmates, of that number sixty-nine were in the camp hospital and seventy-five more were ambulatory, but the hospital could not accommodate them. Ibid., vol. 7:1001.

12. Based on two variables, square footage of available living space at the prison and the largest onetime prison population of 3,000, William Bryant concludes that Cahaba "likely was the most overcrowded of all such Civil War camps, North and South." With 2,000 prisoners, Cahaba afforded each captive 7.5 square feet of living space; with 3,000 prisoners each captive had 5 square feet of living space. Whereas the notorious Andersonville, even "at its peak population of 32,899 in August 1864, still provided an average of 35.7 square feet" of living space. At times, the prison population outnumbered that of the town of Cahaba. See Bryant, *Cahaba Prison*

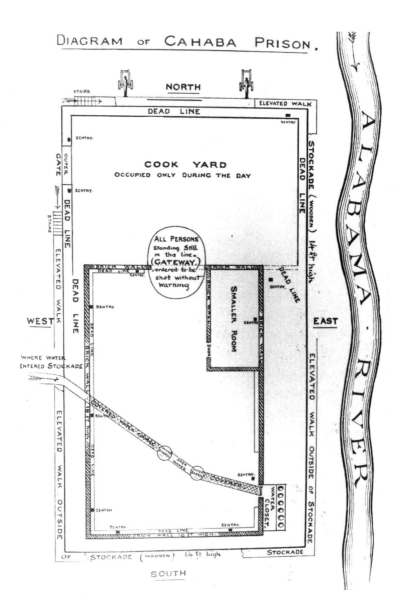

A diagram of Cahaba Prison. Note the Cook Yard, which Adair mentions on October 15, 1864. From Jesse Hawes, *Cahaba: A Story of Captive Boys in Blue* (New York: Burr, 1888), 128–29. Courtesy of Andersonville National Historic Site.

plenty to eat, such as it was. We drew corn meal and either bacon or fresh beef. Lard, salt & sometimes rice and every ten days, one days ration of flour.[13] Here we found the boys of my regt who were captured at Athens.

[October 14] On the 14th some 150 more prisoners were put in here. Crowded as we were before yet still room for more with no prospect of our numbers being diminished soon.[14] Heard by the prisoners who came in that Hood was badly whipped by Thomas.

[October 15] On the 15th had to cook. The yard is so very small and so many have to cook at one time that when all get their fires built it is almost impossible to get around. The fires interspersed throughout the yard. Each one with some one down on their knees blowing their breath away. Trying to get the fires to burn so as to

---

and the Sultana *Disaster,* 2, 52. A more recent study of the Andersonville camp, which accounted for the deadline zone and the swamp area of the sinks, places the living space area at 28 square feet. "Andersonville National Historic Site Employee Handbook," 2007, ANHS.

13. During its initial months of operation, rations at Cahaba appeared to have been adequate. During an early inspection conducted by R. H. Whitfield, the Confederate prison surgeon seemed satisfied with the quality and "punctuality" of the rations served to the prisoners. The prisoners also benefited from a nearby "artesian well" that provided clean water for "drinking, cooking, and bathing, as well as washing." Still, there were sanitation problems. As Whitfield explained, "The privy accommodates but four men at once" is relatively clean, but with "one wheel-barrow to remove filth and other rubbish, there is an unavoidable accumulation of these fruitful sources of disease." *OR,* ser II, vol. 6:1124.

14. Because of the prison's densely populated and closely confined living area, the spread of disease was a major concern. Pneumonia, diarrhea, and dysentery ranked as the three deadliest diseases in the camp. However, a surprisingly small number of prisoners, approximately 225, died of disease at Cahaba. Modern archeological evidence, Confederate records, and federal records all disagree over the exact number of deaths. Nevertheless, the most conservative estimates and the most liberal estimates produce a death rate between 3 and 5 percent, which was a remarkable achievement. The men lacked adequate clothing, rations, and shelter, making it difficult to explain the low death toll. Yet there appeared to have been a sufficient number of doctors assigned to the facility, adequate medical supplies, and a well-maintained prison hospital that operated out of one of the town's old hotels. Bryant, *Cahaba Prison and the* Sultana *Disaster,* 65–66, 73.

cook the food necessary to sustain life, but the case is almost help-less as the wood is green pine, and the only success met with is to make a dense smoke. And yes you can see the poor fellows with tears falling down their cheeks and look around to see what success others meet with. The very picture of dispair. Oh! how I dreaded my cook day to come![15]

[October 15, cont'd.] We were in a mess of 12[16] so that our time to cook, came every six days, two of us cooking at a time. Our mess was composed of Sergt Maj [John M.] Armstrong of the 9th Ind Cav who was a very essential help in the composition of a mess. Next in rank, came the quartermaster sergt of the 111 USCI (John Mader). Then the hospital steward of the 10th Ind Cav whose name is Crawford. Next four 1st sergts of the 111th USCI by name, Lyle G. Adair, John S. Thompson, James H. Hattaway, and William Thomas. One M. Brown of same regiment, weapons [illegible] master John Forbs[?] and one private of the 9th Ind Cav. Then the [illegible] clerk and the regts baker. Then came last but not the *least* a [illegible] from the Emerald Isle P. J. Bundy/Brady[?]. He was the life of the whole prison ever ready with his jokes and not any way particular who was the subject of them.

[October 19] On the 19th there was quite an excitement caused by a number of prisoners being called out for exchange. By their leaving we got a good bunk and plenty of good bed comforts which belonged to the prison.[17] We have succeeded in getting

15. Even Confederate inspectors admitted that "a very insufficient supply of cooking utensils has been furnished [to the prisoners], and there are but three worn-out axes for the use of the whole number." *OR*, ser II, vol. 7:999.

16. One Confederate report filed in October 1864 indicated that messes consisted of ten men. Ibid.

17. Prior to Adair's arrival, the housing accommodations were of an inferior quality. During an early inspection, Confederate prison surgeon R. H. Whitfield reported that the "sleeping arrangements" for the 660 Union prisoners at Cahaba consisted of "rough lumber, without straw or bedding of any kind save the hard plank . . . these bunks, but recently constructed, accommodate but 432 men, so that 228 men are forced to sleep upon the ground." Subsequently, there were an estimated 500 bunks in the prison in a report dated October 16, 1864. Ibid., vol. 6:1124, vol. 7:998.

some good interesting books to read. So that I spend most of my time in reading.[18]

[October 23] This is the Sabbath day. The day to rest from all labor and also the day to attend the house of God and listen to the preaching of God's holy word. We hear the chiming of the church bells as they ring out their melody on the still morning air, but we cannot heed their call for walls & guards surround us on every side.

[October 25] And so time passes slowly to us who are [illegible] within the prison walls until the 25th of Oct when we rec'd a letter from Lieut [Sollayman E.] Fink quartermaster of our regt. It cheered us up greatly to hear from our officers and know that these [illegible] men [illegible] those in the wide world who at least thought of us. The officers were all at Enterprise, Miss and were out on parole of honor to the limits of the town and are boarding at the private houses, and having a better time than prisoners generally do. They also have a house to stay in and make themselves comfortable, how different their situation from ours![19] But why complain, we are in for it, let us bear it like true soldiers who are suffering for the cause of our beloved country which we have espoused.

18. Most of Cahaba's inmates were familiar with Amanda Gardner, the wife of a local railroad contractor who lived just thirty feet from the stockade. She lost her nineteen-year-old son, Cpl. John A. Gardner of Company F of the 5th Alabama, the famed Cahaba Rifles, at the Battle of Seven Pines on May 31, 1862. Yet she harbored no ill will toward the Union prisoners. Gardner furnished the prisoners with homemade remedies, clothing, and food, and she even cut up her carpets so that prisoners could have makeshift blankets and beddings. Most prisoners, however, remembered her extensive book collection, which she willingly shared with the inmates. Her personal library included the complete works of Walter Scott, Charles Dickens, and Edward George Bulwer-Lytton as well as numerous books on history, science, philosophy, religion, and biography. She established a loan system whereby prisoners informed guards of their book request, then she or her young daughter, Belle, delivered the book to the camp, and the guards passed the books on to the prisoners. Books were returned by a similar process. For more on Amanda Gardner, see Bryant, *Cahaba Prison and the* Sultana *Disaster*, 79–84.

19. Also residing in the town of Cahaba were ten paroled federal officers. Their communication with the prison's inmates was monitored closely and followed numerous

[October 29]

Removed from Cahaba

On the morning of the 29th of Oct as the sergt of the prison called out the names of five hundred to go out as we were told for exchange. I could hardly believe my *ears,* when he called the names of part of my regt including my name. Then all was excitement and commotion. The unlucky, as they thought themselves, who had not been called, were giving us letters to send to their friends & loved ones, after we reached the Union lines. Ah! little did they think, we, whose names had been called, would be the last to reach the Union lines of all who were then prisoners. And that many of us were to find our last resting place on the far of rebel [illegible] of Ga, yet such proved to be the case. The day wore slowly away and at sundown we were marched on board the steamer *Cogneth*[?], & started up the Alabama River.

[October 29, cont'd.] How refreshing! it was to once more breathe the [illegible] the air of Heaven and see the beauties of nature brighten up around us. We almost forgot, for the time, the loathsome prison house and the stern realities of war which surrounded us on every side. But when we would look around us we were quickly reminded of it by the grey costumes & the glistening bayonets. We reached Selma by nine o'clock at night, the boat just landed, then passed on. This was the death knell to all our hopes, for had we been going for exchange, we knew we would be taken by way of Vicksburg and would therefore have left the boat at Selma. But alas! how vain the hope! is gone.[20] And we are enveloped in the mid-night darkness

---

restrictions. Their quarters and accommodations were vastly superior to those of the rank and file in the Cahaba camp, and they appeared "satisfied with their treatment." *OR*, ser. II, vol. 7:1000.

20. The Dix-Hill Cartel designated Vicksburg, Mississippi, as the exchange location for prisoners held in the Western Theater. In the east, the cartel initially designated Aiken's Landing on the James River, but two weeks later exchange commissioners changed the location to City Point, Virginia. See Article Seven of the Dix-Hill Cartel in ibid., vol. 4:266–68.

with not one single ray of light to cheer our lonely pilgrimage. How long! Oh how long! will it thus be, is the ache of every heart.

[October 30] We reached Montgomery City, Ala at 2 p.m. on the 30th of Oct 1864. Here we got off the boat & were marched through the old capital of the state, & what was once the capital of the Confederacy. It is a beautiful city, situated on the Ala river and so has the advantages of communication by river, as well as by the railroad. We went into camp to wait 'till Monday morn for the cars.[21] Citizens crowded around the guard line all the evening, anxious to behold with their own eyes, the Yankee vandals who could not fight and who did not know even the [illegible] of five [illegible]. Some were very insulting, while others were, or seemed to sympathize with us & be very solicitous for our welfare.

[October 31] On the 31st left Montgomery on the Macon & Montgomery Rail road. By noon we reached Tallapossa where Gen Rouseau first struck the road in his famous raid. Here we could plainly see the fruits of Yankee labor.[22] Without any incidents worthy of mention we reached Columbus, Ga. Here we lay over night. And quite a number of the prisoners escaped during the night. Previous

21. The Confederacy operated a prison in Montgomery for eight months, from mid-April to December 14, 1862. The guard supervisor was then Cpl. Henry S. Wirz, the same Wirz who would later surface at Andersonville. Conditions at the prison, which was a converted cotton warehouse between Tallapossa Street and the Alabama River, were terrible, and one former Montgomery prisoner recalled that "our rations consisted of a bit of spoiled beef not larger that your two fingers, a small slice of coarse corn-bread without salt and this only twice a day." During the war, 198 Union soldiers died in the Montgomery prison. It is uncertain whether Adair was detained in the original prison or at some other location. Earl Antrim, "Confederate Prison at Montgomery, Ala.," *Alabama Historical Quarterly* 25 (Spring & Summer 1963): 190–96. For more on Montgomery during the Civil War, see John H. Napier III, "Montgomery during the Civil War," *Alabama Review* 41 (Apr. 1988): 103–31.

22. In the summer of 1864, Maj. Gen. Lovell H. Rousseau conducted one of the most successful cavalry raids of the Civil War. His primary target was "the vital industrial complex centering on Selma, Alabama." The July operations resulted in the confiscation of some 42,000 pounds of food supplies such as bacon, sugar, and flour. In addition, Rousseau's men destroyed a number of railroad station buildings,

to my capture I had read in almost any paper I would pick up, the predictions of some army correspondent, describing the destitute condition of the South. And stating that they were on the point of starving out, and could not possibly hold out much longer. Since my capture I have passed the rich farming lands of Miss, over two miles in length, have passed clear across the state of Ala and have seen nothing but plantation after plantation covered with corn & beans, & hundreds of Negroes at work gathering in the crops. It very naturally occurred to my mind that if we had to wait until they starved out, before we were liberated from the prison we would wait until we would grow old and grey.

---

freight cars, and some thirty miles of track between the Alabama towns of Che-haw and Opelika. The repairs to the rail lines took more than a month to complete. Edwin C. Bearss, "Rousseau's Raid on the Montgomery and West Point Railroad," *Alabama Historical Review* 25 (1963): 7, 43; Robert C. Black III, *The Railroads of the Confederacy* (Chapel Hill: Univ. of North Carolina Press, 1952).

CHAPTER 4

Millen

CONFEDERATE OFFICIALS constructed the largest prison used during the war just outside of Millen, Georgia, in the late summer of 1864. Initially, known simply as 79 "due to its approximate distance from Savannah," the development of the town of Millen was tied to Georgia's railroad construction in the 1850s. In 1854, the Central of Georgia Railway completed a line from Savannah to Augusta with a connection at 79. The town was renamed Millen's Junction in honor of McPherson B. Millen, superintendent of the Central of Georgia Railway. By the eve of the Civil War, "a train depot, warehouses, and a hotel" dotted the landscape of the tiny rural town. Oddly enough, Millen was "positioned at almost the exact corner of four very large counties: Bullock, Burke, Emanuel, and Screven," and not until 1905, when the Georgia state legislature created Jenkins County, was the town located in a single county.[1]

The decision to build Millen prison stemmed directly from the crowded conditions at Georgia's most infamous prison, Andersonville. Originally designed to contain 10,000 prisoners, Andersonville held more than 30,000 by midsummer 1864. The crisis there forced Gen. John Winder, commissary general of Richmond prisons as well as all Confederate prisons in Georgia and Alabama, to relieve the

1. Lawton E. Brantley, "Millen," in *New Georgia Encyclopedia,* http://www.georgiaencyclopedia.org/nge/Article.jsp?id=h-2929&hl=y.

beleaguered prison. On July 28, he ordered Captains D. W. Vowles and his son, W. S. Winder, "to select a site for a new prison" and to "secure by rent the land, water privileges, timber, and such houses adjacent as may be thought advisable."[2] Within a week, the captains notified Confederate officials that a site had been selected five miles north of Millen along the Augusta & Savannah Railroad.[3] Just two days after his initial order, Winder informed Samuel Cooper, adjutant and inspector general of the Confederate Army, of the urgency of the situation. "It is very important to build as soon as possible," Winder wrote from his headquarters at Andersonville. "We now have 32,235 prisoners of war." Winder also requested the "authority to press negroes and teams and wagons" as well as the services of a "quartermaster."[4] He correctly anticipated a lack of cooperation from the locals around Millen.[5]

The construction of yet another Confederate prison in Georgia also concerned Gen. Howell Cobb, commander of Georgia's state troops. Aside from Virginia, no state in the Confederacy had more

2. *OR*, ser. II, vol. 7:509.

3. Ibid., 546.

4. Ibid., 514.

5. C. R. Johnson, M.D., of Waynesborough in Burke County formally petitioned the Confederate government to change the location of the prison. In a letter to Secretary of War James Seddon, Johnson argued that "many objections" could be filed against the prison selection site, but he limited himself to two fundamental reasons. First, the doctor claimed that the water supply "inclosed [*sic*] in the stockade" was fed by a spring of "unhealthy, rotten limestone, and no one in our county even thought of drinking it"; therefore, he was "primarily concerned with the health of the prisoners and the guard." Second, the prison site sat at the convergence of several large plantations with "at least 600 or 800 negroes [with]in five miles of it." Johnson made a special entreaty on behalf of a "widow lady" whose bordering plantation was within "half a mile" of the prison grounds. "Her tithe alone last year was 1,300 bushels of corn, 2,500 pounds of bacon, & c.," Johnson reported, and he urged Seddon to find a "more remote" location. He also alleged that "certain parties in the immediate vicinity" of the prison had presented "false representation" to Captain Winder and had done so "entirely for pecuniary purpose." These individuals were "not in the service of the country and never have been, and . . . care nothing for the . . . Government or any one else, so they are putting money in their coffers." See Ibid., 579.

prison sites than Georgia,[6] and of the "thirty-three principal places for the confinement of Union prisoners" Georgia furnished nine, or 27 percent, of the prisons.[7] Consequently, Cobb attempted "to impress" on Confederate secretary of war James Seddon "the importance of preventing" an increase in the number of Confederate prison camps. Cobb worried that much of Georgia was "already too much exposed to raiding parties of the enemy." Moreover, state forces were "small and scarcely able to protect the place, and will become wholly so" if state forces were reassigned as prison guards. Cobb recommended a more equitable distribution "in different states" and warned that an unduly burdened state might be "compelled to obtain from the army in the field a prison guard."[8]

Despite the lack of enthusiasm and cooperation on the state and local levels, Confederate authorities proceeded with the construction of the new prison.[9] By September 5, 1864, some progress had been made, and Adjutant General Cooper questioned Winder as to whether prisoners could be sent to Millen "before completion of the whole prison grounds."[10] Winder arrived at Millen on September 12, and the next day the first prisoners from Andersonville arrived at Millen, although the prison had not been completed.[11] Around the time the prison opened, camp officials as well as some prisoners began to refer to the facility as Camp Lawton in honor of Gen. Alexander Lawton, quartermaster general of the Confederacy. On October 15 Winder announced that "the stockade is completed," and he confidently indicated that Millen

6. Speer, *Portals to Hell,* 332–40. Speer identifies eighty-three Confederate prisons. Virginia's total was 37 percent, and Georgia and Texas both had 13 percent. The only other state above 10 percent was South Carolina at 11 percent.

7. *OR,* ser. II, vol. 8:1004. The much smaller list from the *Official Records* has Virginia supplying 33 percent of the total prisons, Georgia 27 percent, Alabama 12 percent, and the remaining states individually less than 10 percent.

8. Ibid., vol. 7:585–86.

9. Ibid., 593.

10. Ibid., 773.

11. Ibid., 841; George A. Rogers, and R. Frank Saunders Jr., "Camp Lawton Stockade, Millen, Georgia, C.S.A," *Atlanta Historical Journal* 25 (Winter 1981): 84.

could "with great convenience accommodate 32,000 prisoners, and could without inconvenience increase to 40,000."[12] Ultimately, he boasted that the forty-two-acre prison was "the largest prison in the world."[13] Adair arrived roughly two months after the prison opened, on the morning of November 2.

Most relocated prisoners from Andersonville preferred the accommodations and treatment that they received at Millen to their previous experience. Still, Camp Lawton was not completely free from danger. Apparently, a prison gang similar to the legendary Raiders of Andersonville formed at Camp Lawton. Although incidents of abuse never reached an alarming regularity at Millen, a rather large melee did occur one day and resulted in the arrest of several gang members. Ultimately, the rebellious Union prisoners spent "a day and night" in the stocks, "and when released they joined the rebel army, entering the artillery that manned the guns in the fort covering the prison."[14] Certainly disease, the cumulative effects of malnutrition, and exposure made survival more difficult, and, "according to various contemporary accounts," one historian has suggested that "there might have been as many as seven hundred deaths" at Camp Lawton.[15] Based on the only set of official returns from the camp, the death rate at Millen was not quite 5 percent, well below the 15.5 percent of Union soldiers who died in Southern prisons but reflective of the difficulty of prison camp life under any circumstances.[16]

[November 1] Left Columbus at five o'clock. Nothing worthy of note until we reached Fort Valley where the road heading to Anderson-

12. Despite the declaration, Winder acknowledged in his reports that they had just that same day begun construction on the camp's hospitals. *OR*, ser. II, vol. 7:993.

13. Ibid., 869–70.

14. Roy Meredith, ed., *This Was Andersonville by John McElroy* (1879; repr., New York: Fairfax Press, 1957), 209.

15. Speer, *Portals to Hell*, 279.

16. *OR*, ser. II, vol. 7:1113–14.

ville intersected the Columbus & Macon Rail road. Here we heard the report that we were to go to Andersonville prison and from the reports we had heard of that place, we of course dreaded the very idea of our making our entrance there. What terrible suspense! was that which was endured while lying there at Fort Valley. Anxious to start yet fearing we would take the road to that most loathsome of all prisons, Andersonville. At last we start, we near the switch of the Andersonville road, we pass it, every ear is anxiously listening with throbbing hearts, the signal from the engineer to back & switch off on the fatal road. But no we get faster and faster, we are enabled to draw a long breath we involuntarily exclaimed, *Thank God!* We are free from the fate of the present at least.[17]

[November 1, cont'd.] Just as the sun was sinking in the western horizon we reached Macon. In passing through the streets of this place the train ran very slowly and the little boys congregated along the road & threw stones & sticks, or anything they could get hold of at the prisoners sometimes seriously threatening the lives of the prisoners. We switched off on the Atlanta & Savannah road. It is now near dark and very cloudy but still not half so dark and cloudy as are our prospects for the future. We now found we were doomed to travel during the night, and that, on flat, open dirt cars with a strong prospect of rain but we try to make ourselves as comfortable as possible. By nine o'clock it commenced raining, miserable indeed was our condition now, a cold steady rain, and we without a single thing to protect us from it.

17. As early as 1862, there were prisoner reminiscences depicting the horrors of Richmond's warehouse prisons. In early 1863, the U.S. Sanitary Commission issued a report condemning the treatment of Northern prisoners. By midsummer 1864, Northern newspapers carried numerous stories about the atrocities at Andersonville Prison. The public awareness had been fueled by the congressional Committee on the Conduct of the War, which in May 1864 simultaneously released separate reports, one condemning the Confederate actions at Fort Pillow and the other for the mistreatment of Northern prisoners, especially those who had been confined at

[November 2] Thus we traveled until three o'clock in the morning. When we reached Millen Station. As we got off the cars & had to stand in the rain until daylight. After daylight we were marched over to the prison, which was about a quarter of a mile from the station. As we gained the brow of a hill the prison presented itself to our view in all of its horrors.

[November 2, cont'd.]

Our Entrance into Millen Prison

It was formed of pine logs hewed & set some four feet in the ground, side by side, the top ends extending some eighteen feet above the ground, with sentry boxes on them at the distance of about thirty paces apart, this enclosing about forty acres, inside this enclosure, thirty feet, was a railing called a deadline.[18] But it was in many places torn away so that the prisoners could not tell where the lines had formerly been.[19] We were drawn up in line outside the gate, and the roll called. The rain came down in torrents, we were drenched to the skin. I and my comrades were in the first hundred called out.

Andersonville. Adair's apprehension was somewhat misplaced, because only those too sick to travel, fewer than a thousand, remained at Andersonville in early November 1864; most had been relocated in anticipation of a federal liberation raid, which never happened. See William B. Hesseltine, "The Propaganda Literature of Civil War Prisons," *Journal of Southern History* 1 (Feb. 1935): 56–66; William B. Hesseltine, "Andersonville Revisited," *Georgia Review* 10 (Spring 1956): 92–100; Ovid Futch, *History of Andersonville Prison* (Gainesville: Univ. Press of Florida, 1968), 116–17; Bruce Tap, *Over Lincoln's Shoulder: The Committee on the Conduct of the War* (Lawrence: Univ. Press of Kansas, 1998), 203.

18. According to a report filed by Union general John W. Geary, commander of the 2nd Division, Twentieth Corps, who arrived at Camp Lawton a few weeks after the Confederates abandoned the prison, "the stockade was about 800 feet square, and inclosed nearly fifteen acres. It was made of heavy pine logs, at intervals of some eighty yards were placed sentry boxes. Inside of the stockade, running parallel to it at a distance from it of thirty feet, was a fence of light scantling, supported on short posts. This was the 'dead line.'" *OR*, ser. I, vol. 44:274.

19. One prisoner recalled that no Union soldiers were shot during his six weeks at Millen, "a circumstance simply remarkable since I do not recall a single week passed anywhere else without at least one murder by the guards." Meredith, *This Was Andersonville*, 207.

And on account of our being in a colored regt nothing was mean enough for them to call us, an no cursing *hard* enough.

[November 2, cont'd.] A sergt was appointed to draw rations for the hundred, and we were then marched through the gate. Oh horror of horrors! The sight that met our eyes! on our entrance to the prison. Just to the right of the gate, as we entered, lay the lifeless forms of some sixty Union prisoners. As one gazed upon the faces of those martyred dead, who were lying there without the shadows of a garment to cover their nakedness from the wicked gaze of their relentless foes. Our hearts sank within us, for said we to ourselves, God only knows how soon we may be lying there in the cold embraces of death.[20] The rain continued all day, by paying half a dollar in silver, we got a few sticks with which to put up our blankets and thus forming a shelter for us from the rain. Oh! the gloom that pervaded our hearts that day! How sensitively did we realize the truth of that hymn "Be it ever so humble, there is no place like home."[21] As we thought of home and friends, and all that was near and dear to us; that we had sacrificed on the altar of our country. And then we turned our thoughts to our present condition. Is it then strange, that we should sigh for liberty, and almost give up in despair?[22]

20. Millen commandant Capt. D. W. Vowels filed the camp's only set of prison returns on November 8, 1864. Based on the lone population report, the death rate at that time was roughly 5 percent, derived from 10,229 prisoners received and 486 deaths. See *OR*, ser. II, vol. 7:1113. According to Pvt. John McElroy, Company L, 16th Illinois Cavalry, "one man in every ten died," or roughly 700 men. Neither Adair nor Pvt. M. J. Umsted, Company A, 13th Iowa Infantry, recorded the arrival of additional prisoners after November 8. In fact, both men noted the departure of prisoners. Thus, 700 dead out of a population of 10,229 produces a death rate of almost 7 percent. The death rate in Confederate prisons was 28 percent. See M. J. Umsted Diary, Andersonville Diary Collection (hereafter ADC), ANHS; Meredith, *This Was Andersonville*, 216.

21. For the importance of this hymn, see Ernest L. Abe, "Home, Sweet Home: A Civil War Soldier's Favorite Song," *America's Civil War* (May 1996): 12, 78, 80.

22. The famed prison polemicist John L. Ransom, a sergeant in the 9th Michigan Cavalry, arrived at Camp Lawton the day before Adair, having previously been held at Andersonville when overcrowding and death rates reached their highest levels. The sergeant of the 9th Michigan Cavalry was quick to draw distinctions between

[November 4] Continued raining all day yesterday, in the evening got out for wood and later in the evening moved to the part of the prison assigned us for encampment. Howard James McChan of my old co here, he was taken prisoner at Atlanta Ga. Cleared off last night and is quite cool this morning. Went to work fixing up a place to stay, have a very comfortable place compared with what many have. Was very much surprised and sorely grieved to see so many of our men treat the oath so lightly which they had taken to protect, support, and defend the government of the United States, under the protection of which they were born and reared. And now when the next opportunity is offered, they volunteer and take an oath to support and defend the enemies of their father country.[23] And thus forgive themselves and disgrace their friends and relations and the name of soldier. For they cannot be true soldiers and thus prove false to their colors.[24]

---

the two prison facilities. "The stockade is similar to that at Andersonville," Ransom noted, "but in a more settled country, the ground high and grassy, and through the prison runs a stream of good, pure water, with no swamp at all. It is apparently a pleasant healthy location." Ransom also appreciated the fallen timber within the stockade, which had been left for the prisoners to build "shanties and places to sleep in," a fortuitous circumstance that Adair would soon appreciate. John Ransom, *Andersonville Diary: Escape and List of Dead* (1881; repr., New York: Haskell House, 1974), 156, 159.

23. Most prison camps lacked the military personnel necessary for routine operations. In order to fill this void, camp authorities offered Union prisoners the opportunity to work as hospital stewards, woodcutters, cooks, or undertakers—hence, the appellation Galvanized Rebels. In exchange for this so-called privilege, the prisoners had to pledge an oath that they would not attempt to escape and demonstrate a loyalty to the Confederate cause, which earned them the nickname by some Union prisoners of Oath Men. Some Galvanized Rebels were even willing to fight for the Confederate Army rather than remain in captivity. The exact number of men who became Galvanized Rebels cannot be accurately determined because the Confederate prisons did not submit monthly population returns. The exception to that rule was Andersonville Prison, but even in those cases where population reports existed, the classifications, "paroled, released, or exchanged," were imprecise and often generated confusion. See *OR*, ser. II, vol. 8:1004.

24. Pvt. M. J. Umsted indicated that fifty-two soldiers took the oath on that day. Umsted Diary, Nov. 4, 1864.

[November 5] Bought a pine log about eight feet long and two feet thick for eight-dollars in greenbacks. This being split thin, then by planting two posts in the ground and laying a pole on the top of the posts, we then placed an end of the thin split pieces on the ground and one end in the hole. This we then covered over one foot in depth with earth. We then sodded up the ends and also built a sod chimney. And by digging out the inside to the depth of two feet, we had a very comfortable house for six of us to live in, namely Jno S Thompson, Jas Hattaway, John Meder, Wm Thomas, Jas McChan, and L. Adair. We just had room to all lie down at night. But we were content with that. Rebel papers state that arrangements have been made for the exchange of ten thousand prisoners.

[November 8] Day of President Election; held an election in the prison, went strong for Lincoln, out of 4,774 Lincoln got 989 majority.[25] When men who are kept in prison and are enduring such hardships and suffering will vote for Lincoln, what must be the issue in the army and with the people in the North. Our rations are very limited, a little meal, a few beans, and sometimes a little rice or hominy, and generally a little mouthful of fresh beef. And once in a while sweet potatoes instead of meal.[26]

[November 10] The rebel ladies of the vicinity visited Camp Lawton today to furnish the rebel soldiers with clothing. We could see them from our quarters in the prison.

25. Adair's outcome is mathematically impossible. Most likely, Lincoln received 2,882 votes to McClellan's 1,892, which would have given the president a 990 majority, or 60 percent of the vote. Umsted recorded 2,777 votes for Lincoln and 1,845 for McClellan, a total of 4,622 votes, which gave Lincoln a 932 vote majority, or 60 percent of the vote. Umsted Diary, Nov. 8, 1864. For more on the election, see Glenn Robins, "Race, Repatriation, and Galvanized Rebels: Union Prisoners and the Exchange Question in Deep South Prison Camps," *Civil War History* 53 (June 2007): 126–30.

26. Generally speaking, the prisoners viewed the rations as vastly superior to Andersonville and regarded Captain Vowels as a fair-minded prison commandant. Ransom, *Andersonville Diary*, 160–61. Fellow prisoner John McElroy agreed with Ransom regarding the rations and Vowles. Meredith, *This Was Andersonville*, 207.

[November 11] Quite an excitement in prison today, rebel recruiting officers are in, offering to take out any who will volunteer, provided their time is out in the Miss Army, got some two hundred recruits to day.[27]

[November 14] Yesterday and today everything is excitement, the doctors have been examining the sick, and taking out [prisoners] for exchange. Prisoners who have plenty of greenbacks can, by paying from fifty to one hundred dollars, buy their way out. It is hoped by the prisoners that this is a general exchange.[28]

[November 16] Some rebel prisoners, who have been exchanged came to Lawton last night. They say it is a general exchange, and they also state that Lincoln is elected.

[November 18] Took some two hundred prisoners out for exchange today. Some were stout and hearty looking fellows, while some were weak and emaciated and hardly able to walk alone. They are cutting down our rations daily, we barely get enough for one meal now.[29]

27. Umsted estimated a higher number of Galvanized Rebels: "quite a few (say 300)." Umsted Diary, Nov. 11, 1864.

28. Even Confederate authorities confirmed the heinous auctioning of passes for parole. On hearing of alleged improprieties, Gen. John Winder "instituted [an] inquiry" of Camp Lawton commandant Captain Vowles. "But the evidence of prisoners not being acceptable," the report stated, "the charge was not sustained, although $60 paid by a prisoner was recovered from a clerk in Vowles's office. The suspicion was so great against this officer that General Winder declared he should have no such command in the future." *OR*, ser. II, vol. 8:765. Umsted described the bribery scandal as more widespread. He priced parole passes at $50 per prisoner and estimated that "the officers received sixty or seventy-five thousand from the men of the camp. Umsted Diary, Nov. 19, 1864.

29. Ransom had a slightly different recollection, especially with respect to the number of Galvanized Rebels who left the camp: "Food given us in smaller quantities, and hurriedly so, too. All appears to be in a hurry. Cloudy, and rather wet weather, and getting decidedly cooler . . . recruiting officers among us trying to induce prisoners to enter their army. Say it is not exchange for during the war, and half a dozen desert, and go with them. Even if we are not exchanged during the war, don't think we will remain prisoners long." Ransom, *Andersonville Diary*, 170–71.

[November 19] It is reported by one of the guards that Sherman is on this side of Macon and moving in this direction, god speed him on his way, and may he be successful in liberating us from our thralldom, is the prayer of all prisoners.

[November 21] Yesterday they came in to call out more prisoners, took mostly old prisoners, and little boys. Last night, about midnight the eight div was ordered out to leave, the rain was just pouring down in torrents. We marched to the gate where we had to stand a good half hour in the rain before we got out. We were then marched to the depot, and got on board the train.

CHAPTER 5

Blackshear and Thomasville

BLACKSHEAR

MOST PRISONERS LIKELY HAD mixed emotions when they learned on November 14, 1864, that they were being removed from Camp Lawton. Just four days earlier, Gen. William T. Sherman began what would become known as his March to the Sea. Confederate officials feared that one of Sherman's objectives may have been the liberation of prison camps. Sherman's men did arrive at Millen on December 3; however, they found no prisoners. The Confederates had removed all prisoners by November 25. Sherman ordered that the town of Millen Junction be burned; he then proceeded toward Savannah.[1] While the prisoners enjoyed the news and rumors of Sherman's success, the uncertainty associated with yet another removal certainly tempered their excitement. Indeed, to avoid Sherman's advancing army, the Confederate authorities chaotically shuffled Union prisoners of war throughout the Deep South and hastily erected several new prisons in southern Georgia. These "barren stockades" were little more than "open areas or fields surrounded by guard details."[2]

Blackshear was a small and relatively poor community in Pierce County. For most of its history, Pierce County, which was named

---

1. Rogers and Saunders, "Camp Lawton Stockade, Millen," 85.
2. Speer, *Portals to Hell,* 340.

in honor of the fourteenth U.S. president, Franklin Pierce, was an untamed frontier. As late as 1850, local residents recalled that "this county was thinly peopled . . . and schools were difficult to find . . . teachers were scarce . . . the farms were small . . . and there was but little cotton." They also remembered "there were no railroads then, nor . . . a single framed house in Pierce County. The Georgia legislature did not incorporate the county until December 1857. The 1860 federal census, the first conducted in the county, indicated a total population of 1,973, with 319 residing in the county seat of Blackshear. Thus, residents did not use exaggerated language when they described their region as a "wilderness." As someone recollected in 1890, "Robinson Crusoe would have felt perfectly at home in Pierce County in those days."[3]

Confusion and disarray characterized both the decision to locate and to build a Confederate prison at Blackshear in southeast Georgia. The only logic behind the selection of the location was the town's proximity to a significant rail line. On May 1, 1859, the Atlantic & Gulf (formerly known as the Savannah, Albany, & Gulf) completed a station at Blackshear; ultimately, nineteen stations were built between Savannah and Thomasville. Miller's Station outside of Savannah was No. 1, Blackshear No. 8, and Thomasville No. 19.[4] Despite the convenient access to the railroad, Blackshear commander Col. Henry Forno disclosed numerous problems in his first report on the new prison. "I have been in a state of uncertainty ever since I came here," Forno advised Gen. John Winder, and have had "great difficulty in obtaining supplies."[5] The first prisoners arrived at Blackshear on November 16, three weeks before Forno filed the report. By December 1 the camp population had exceeded 5,000 and included Lyle Adair, who arrived on November 24.[6]

3. Dean Broome, comp., *History of Pierce County Georgia* (Blackshear, Ga.: Broome Printing and Office Supplies, 1973), 1–4, 6, 183, 201, 182, 184.
4. Ibid., 255, 252, 254, 198.
5. *OR*, ser. II, vol. 7:1204.
6. Speer, *Portals to Hell*, 279.

Although he recalled few specifics about his brief imprisonment at Blackshear, Pvt. John McElroy, Company L, 16th Illinois Cavalry, provided a colorful and highly sarcastic composite of the South Georgia community. "We were informed that we were at Blackshear, the county seat of Pierce County," McElroy wrote, "where they kept the Court House or 'county seat' is beyond conjecture to me, since I could not see a half-dozen houses in the whole clearing and not one of them was a respectable dwelling, taking even so low a standard . . . as that afforded to the majority of Georgia houses." He further derided the region when he speculated on the county's ability to sustain a local population: "I was not astonished to learn that it took five hundred square miles of Pierce County land to maintain two thousand 'crackers' even as poorly as they lived. I should fully want that much of it to support one fair-sized Northern family as it should be." In McElroy's mind, the dominant feature of the Pierce County landscape were "a few 'razor-back' hogs, a species so gaunt and thin that I heard a man once declare that he stopped a lot belonging to a neighbor from crawling through the cracks of a tight board fence by tying a knot in their tails." According to McElroy, the razorback hogs roamed "the woods and supply all the meat used" in the county.[7]

McElroy judged the camp at Blackshear as "very favorable for escape," and he considered reaching the seacoast, "not more than forty miles away," as a distinct possibility. But most prisoners, McElroy among them, did not stay at Blackshear long enough to execute an escape.[8] Indeed, some prisoners left Blackshear shortly after their arrival, but their brief stay and subsequent relocation represented yet another chapter in their ever-changing captivity stories.

[November 21, cont'd.] The rations were put on the cars, and issued to the men. They consisted of two hard tack, and a small piece of meat. By five o'clock in the evening, we reached Savannah, Ga, where we changed from the Atlanta and Macon road, to the Savannah,

---

7. Meredith, *This Was Andersonville*, 225–26.
8. Ibid., 226.

Albany, and Gulf road. Here we were put on open flat cars. We lay there until ten o'clock at night. It now quit raining and had turned very cold. Oh! the suffering of that night! The thoughts of it even at this distant day causes me to shudder. We traveled all night and just as the sun was rising we stopped at Blackshear Station got off the train and built fires by which we warmed our [illegible] limbs.

[November 23] Rations came today the first we have had since we left Millen.[9] But we only drew crackers.[10] No clue as yet to what they intend doing with us. But the Rebel officers tell us we were brought here for exchange. But we fear that we will be doomed to disappointment in this respect.

[November 24] Very cool this morning, and last night. Another train load of prisoners came up last night. This morning moved out into the pine woods about one mile from Blackshear Station. Another train load of prisoners comes in this evening.

9. Pvt. W. B. Smith, Company K, 14th Illinois, painted a scene of utter desperation on his arrival at Blackshear: "All I had eaten since leaving Savannah was the three or four palmetto buds secured along the way, and a turnip top which a guard had thrown away; and when we arrived at Blackshear I was almost exhausted from hunger and cold; and was but barely able to march out to camp; and there we were kept twenty-four hours longer without a morsel to eat. In the endeavor to appease our hunger we split up pieces of fat pine wood into splinters, boiled these in our buckets and cups, and skimmed off the resin which raised to the top, and chewed it for gum. This was evidently an injury to us, and in many instances was followed by severe pain." W. B. Smith, *On Wheels and How I Came There: Giving the Personal Experiences and Observations of a Fifteen-Year-Old Yankee Boy as a Soldier and Prisoner in the American Civil War* (New York: Hunt & Eaton, 1893), 257–58.

10. Pvt. William H. Lightcap, 14th Illinois, provided a fuller description of the first rations received at Blackshear: "One would naturally think they would be inclined to give us some extra on account of being so long without food, but they started at the head of our line and gave but two crackers to each and nothing but the two crackers. I stood near the head of the line and when I received my quota I stepped behind as some others did, sneaked down the line and fell in again. I trembled slightly for fear they had noticed me, because for a trifle like that they would severely punish me. I got two more crackers which so encouraged me that I tried it again and got in all six. Some may have done better but a very great majority got but two." William H. Lightcap, *The Horrors of Southern Prisons During the War of the Rebellion* (Platteville, Wisc.: Journal Job, 1902), 61.

[November 26] Yesterday was busy fixing up quarters, today there was one thousand called out and paroled after which they were sent to Savannah, as were told for exchange.

[November 28] The sergts of the hundreds, drew cuts to day to see whose hundreds should go out next, those who went out yesterday evening came back this evening, having only got as far as the depot on account of not being able to get transportation.

[November 30] Have been very unwell for several days, hardly about to get about. Yesterday was pretty near all day having [illegible] call quartermaster says he has been issuing some six hundred rations more than he has prisoners, my thousand is ordered to be in readiness to night to leave for Savannah. It is quite warm, the frogs sing like it was Spring. The prisoners are in pretty good heart thinking we will soon get out and be enabled to once more return to home and friends.

[December 2] Yesterday lay all day expecting to be called out. But disappointment seemed to be our lot. We did not draw any rations today. The men are getting very uneasy fearing we are going to be consigned to another prison instead of to our own lines. Five prisoners were brought in this evening who had escaped and were recaptured. They say the rebs are taking out of Savannah. Sherman and his army are near. Savannah [illegible] to the Union Army.[11]

[December 5] Yesterday, the rebel officer of the day, said that Sherman took Savannah after three hours of fighting. Was ordered out

11. Pvt. Lessel Long, 13th Indiana, believed the false exchanges were part of a deception plan to relax prisoners and discourage escapes. The Confederates ultimate objective, according to Long, was to relocate the prisoners to Charleston or Florence, South Carolina, before Gen. Judson Kilpatrick could breach the Charleston & Savannah Railroad. He also indicated that security at Blackshear increased significantly after the former parolees returned. Lessel Long, *Twelve Months in Andersonville: On the March—in the Battle—in the Rebel Prison Pens, and at Last in God's Country* (Huntington, Ind.: Thad & Mark Butler, 1886), 113–14.

this morning in readiness to march. Sixteen hundred of us were taken out & marched down to the station. Here we drew hard tack for two days. Were then put on board the cars, and traveled until after night. The train was stopped and we had to lay in the crowded cars all night. Just imagine how seventy-five or one hundred men, crowded into a box car, put in the time of two days and one night, the time we had to spend on board that train and in that crowded state, and you will then have some idea of what we had to endure.

THOMASVILLE

On December 7, Blackshear commander Col. Henry Forno estimated that the prison's population had been reduced from 5,000 to 2,500 prisoners.[12] By December 11 Blackshear had been completely evacuated. Some of the prisoners had been removed to Savannah and then on to Charleston and Florence, South Carolina. Others, including Lyle Adair, were being relocated to yet another newly constructed open stockade in Thomasville, Georgia.[13] Thomas County, Georgia, the former Creek and Apalachee Indian hunting ground in the southwest part of the state, was surrounded by such waterways as the Chattahoochee, Okefenokee, Ocmulgee, and upper Altamaha rivers. In 1825, local resident Thomas J. Johnson introduced a bill in the Georgia legislature that created Thomas County, and Thomasville became the county seat.[14] Thomas County farmers produced significant amounts of cotton, sugar cane, rice, and corn, and their state ranks by county in these four areas was thirty-second, third, ninth, and fortieth, respectively.[15] Population figures indicate that in 1860 Thomas County had a white population of 4,488 and a slave population of 6,244 (58 percent), whereas

12. *OR*, ser. II, vol. 7:1204.

13. Speer, *Portals to Hell*, 280.

14. William Warren Rogers, *Ante-Bellum Thomas County: 1825–1861* (Tallahassee: Florida State Univ. Press, 1963), 1–3, 10, 5.

15. The total value of cash farms in 1860 was $1,530,540. The state rankings in crop production are based on the average ranks 1840–1860. Ibid., 51–55.

the state totals were 591,588 whites and 462,198 slaves (44 percent). The significance of slavery in Thomas County would clearly shape its political culture.[16]

As the secession convention convened in Georgia, among those voting for an ordinance of secession were three delegates from Thomas County.[17] When the Confederacy issued a call to arms, the county matched the secessionist fervor by forming a number of militia companies. Indeed, "few Georgia counties furnished more companies or men [for military service] in proportion to their population." While the war waged on the front lines, Thomas Countians worked feverously to maintain the home front. By 1864, however, the strain of war produced inflation and shortages. As a result of the deteriorating financial situation, "Thomasville had more than the usual quota of fleeing persons." With convenient access to the Atlantic & Gulf rail line, local residents exited the community at a "feverish" pace in late 1864 and early 1865, about the time of the creation of the Thomasville prison. For those who remained, they endured additional hardships caused by "more than fifty Confederate deserters who descended on the county and overwhelmed the local police."[18]

The first prisoners arrived at Thomasville from Blackshear on December 5, 1864, under the supervision of Col. James H. Fannin. Shortly thereafter, Col. Henry Forno dispersed an additional 1,200 prisoners to join Colonel Fannin some 200 miles due west along the Atlantic & Gulf Railroad. The change in scenery appealed to many of the prisoners. "Thomasville was a pretty town located on high ground," remembered Pvt. William H. Lightcap, Company K, 14th Illinois Volunteer Infantry. "The surrounding country was beautiful, a nice view south, east, and west, but north covered with fine timber." Even the location of the prison, a mile or so north of the

16. Ibid., 56–57, 50, 68–69, 61.

17. Ibid., 118–19.

18. William Warren Rogers, *Thomas County During the Civil War* (Tallahassee: Florida State Univ. Press, 1964), 9–15, 1, 75, 92, 99.

town, Lightcap found appealing: "We were taken beyond the town
. . . close to the timber on a fine grassy knoll."[19] Fellow prisoner Pvt.
Lessel Long, Company F, 13th Indiana Infantry, agreed: "This was a
much better part of the country than we had left. The town seemed
to have some life."[20] As for the camp conditions, Private Lightcap
made the obvious, and yet revealing, comment about the lack of
Confederate preparedness: "It was evident that they never thought of
taking us to Thomasville before they were cut from South Carolina,
or they certainly would have started at least to build a pen of some
kind to keep us in."[21]

During their confinement at Thomasville, Union prisoners benefited from favorable weather conditions and a constant supply of
wood. Based on prisoner accounts, rations appeared to be adequate
but lacking in variety.[22] Aside from their initial observations, few
prisoners recorded substantive commentary on the prison. Lessel
Long, after recalling his first impressions, wrote in his memoir, "We
did not stop at Thomasville more than ten or twelve days until we
were informed that we would go back to Andersonville."[23] Without
question, the temporal character of Thomasville Prison was clear to
both prisoner and captor. As historian William Marvel writes, "On
December 11, after most of the Blackshear prisoners had reached
Thomasville, conscripted gangs of slaves started shoveling out the
ditch lines for another stockade. For five days they bent their backs
to the work, but they had not even begun to raise the walls when
the imminent fall of Savannah convinced Confederate authorities to
give up this cantonment, too."[24] Adair's confinement at Thomasville
lasted thirteen days.

19. Lightcap, *The Horrors of Southern Prisons*, 63.
20. Long, *Twelve Months in Andersonville*, 123.
21. Lightcap, *The Horrors of Southern Prisons*, 63.
22. Smith, *On Wheels*, 262.
23. Long, *Twelve Months in Andersonville*, 123.
24. William Marvel, *Andersonville: The Last Depot* (Chapel Hill: Univ. of North
Carolina Press, 1994), 226.

[December 6] Started on early this morning. Two of my messmates jumped from the cars and attempted to escape. But were both captured, not however until one of them was shot through the hip by a musket ball.[25] Reached Thomasville just about sunset, late in the evening it commenced raining. Were marched out about one mile from Town, and went into camp.[26] Continually raining all night. We just got some bark and lay down to keep us out of the mud, then covered up with our blankets & slept as soundly all night, as if we had been on a bed of down.

[December 7] On the 7th got out and got some poles to fix us up a shelter & some wood for fires.

[December 8] Drew yesterday's & to day's rations of meal. So we have plenty today after fasting yesterday. I am quite unwell have a severe attack of camp diarrhea. Weather still cloudy and unpleasant. But warm for December.

25. Private Lightcap provided a more sinister picture of a foiled escape. "On the road to Thomasville, in the night, a few jumped off the cars. About a week after one was brought in and he was the worst looking sight I ever saw. The citizens got after him with blood hounds and pressed him so closely that he had to climb a tree. He was beyond the reach of the hounds but when the citizens came up they commanded him to come down. He said he would if they would call off the hounds and protect him, which they promised to do. As soon as he alighted one of them knocked him down with the butt of his gun, which blow knocked one eye out and then let the hounds bite and pull him round until they were satisfied. I do not believe it is the least exaggeration to state that there was not a spot on his body larger than the palm of a man's hand that was not marked by a dog's tooth. He swore vengeance on those citizens if he lived to the close of the war." See Lightcap, *The Horrors of Southern Prisons*, 64.

26. Private Smith described the prison site as a "square inclosure of four or five acres, covered with heavy pine timber." Surrounding the prison was "a deep, wide ditch," which Smith estimated "was five or six feet deep and too wide for us to jump across." The Confederates, who impressed slave labor to construct the facility, used the extracted dirt to form embankments around the prison, where guards equipped with artillery were posted for security purposes. Smith, *On Wheels*, 261. The completed work impressed Private Long: "It formed a pretty good breast-work. The guards walked on top of the ridge. The artillery was planted at suitable places. There was a heavy guard kept around us all the time." Long, *Twelve Months in Andersonville*, 123.

[December 9] Still very unwell, we had a hard steady rain, rained all night. But we managed to keep dry. Have been so unwell that I lay in bed all day to day. It has rained off & on all day. Drew two days rations on the 10th eat baked sweet potatoes, as we drew meal, beef, salt, & sweet potatoes. Was the first meal I have relished since I have been sick.[27]

[December 11] The remainder of the prisoners came in from Blackshear last night.[28] Is very cold and windy to day.

[December 12] Was quite cool. Last night Sam Champman & I got out and set down a large tree some three feet through, the only ax we had to use was worn off until the edge was at least one quarter inch in thickness. We were just half a day cutting it down.

[December 13] Quite cool for the sunny South. When I waked up this morning every thing was covered with frost. Had roll call this morn, had to stand in line nearly all the afternoon,[29] got out in the evening to get wood.

27. At roughly the same time that Adair complained of poor health due to severe diarrhea, Lightcap stated that a smallpox epidemic swept through the camp killing 500 prisoners. Adair's omission of such an occurrence suggests the death toll was not that high. Lightcap did, however, reveal how vulnerable the men were to health crises: "Sleeping on the damp ground, without shelter, care or medicine, [Thomasville] was not a desirable place." Lightcap, *The Horrors of Southern Prisons,* 63–64. Historian William Warren Rogers believed that Lightcap "undoubtedly exaggerated" the total number of dead. Still, the numbers of sick prisoners was significant enough to require the assistance of the local community. The First Methodist Church in Thomasville served as a temporary hospital, as did the Fletcher Institute, the "town's leading school." The community's humanitarian support also included burying dead prisoners in the Methodist church cemetery. Rogers, *Thomas County During the Civil War,* 87.

28. On December 7, just two days after the first arrivals and just one day after Adair's arrival, the prison population reached 2,500 inmates; ultimately Thomasville received 5,000 prisoners. Smith, *On Wheels,* 262.

29. Private Umsted was extremely irritated by his captors' inefficiency: "Fell into the ranks for roll call at 8:00 a.m. and got through a little before 1:00 p.m. the Johnny's are the slowest and most ignorant set of beings I ever saw, always take the most tiresome and slowest route for everything." Umsted Diary, Dec. 13, 1864.

[December 14] Went to work and fixed up a shed and covered it with pine boughs, did not have quite enough. It commenced raining and rained most of the evening. Then cleared off and was very pleasant during the night.

[December 15] Got out this morning and got enough boughs to finish covering our houses, so that we are very comfortably fixed up now. A number of ladies came out from the city to indulge themselves in a good look at the Yankee vandals. One of the guards threatened to shoot me. And all I dared to do was to look the guard defiantly in the eye and grit my teeth which I did with a vengeance.

[December 16] Took us out by hundreds and organized us, as they found they had been issuing to some four or five hundred more prisoners than they had. We then drew large rations for two days.[30]

[December 17] Had a general wash & cleaning up, as the citizens of Thomasville were kind enough to present the prisoners with some soap. This evening drew two days rations of hard tack and salt. Rumors in camp of another move.

[December 18] Had a big breakfast this morning and drew one day's rations of meal & beef. There is a great talk in camp of our leaving here soon. We have orders to save the hard tack issued us. Weather very warm.

30. Some resourceful prisoners, such as Private Smith, employed a technique known as flanking to secure more rations. At Thomasville, prison guards dispersed rations from the back of a wagon. Smith remembered, "As we passed by each man was handed three crackers . . . when I drew mine I put them in my blouse pocket. Then I broke ranks, managed to elude the guards . . . dropped into the lines again . . . [and] I received three more crackers." The Illinois private successfully flanked the ration line twice and with his initial allotment secured a total of nine crackers. He admitted, however, that this flanking incident was his lone success during his entire captivity, although he "tried it many times." Smith, *On Wheels*, 262.

[December 19] Got orders this morning to be ready in half an hour to leave. Left Thomasville on the Albany road, marched about ten miles when we went into camp for the night, has been very warm today. Late this evening just before we went into camp a rebel soldier, who had been in prison on Johnston's Island,[31] was standing at the road side. He had been paroled & was home on furlough. When he saw us marching along, the tears rolled down his cheeks, and said he, "Boys, I had no idea our men treated *you* in this manner," "When your men had me a prisoner I was treated well, had plenty to eat, and good shelter." Poor fellow! He was having the scales knocked from his eyes, so that he might see the error of his ways.[32]

[December 20] Marched some 15 miles to day, starting at daybreak. We did not get into camp until late at night. Had to wade a large stream just before we went into camp. We drew rations of hard tack and beef.

[December 21] Rained nearly all night. Had a very uncomfortable night of it. Started at daylight. We were in the advances, under the command of Maj Burks of the 4th Georgia Militia. He was a very tyrannical man, would not allow us to go two steps out of the road to avoid water. The consequence was we just had to wade, wade, wade,

31. This was an intriguing encounter. Johnson's Island Prison was located one mile offshore in Sandusky Bay, Lake Erie, and near the town of Sandusky, Ohio. From early 1863, Johnson's Island had at minimum 2,000 prisoners; by early 1864 it had 2,300 prisoners, but only fifty-nine were not officers. Despite frigid temperatures, Johnson's Island "was considered then to be one of the best of the Union prisons, with good barracks and a low death rate." Heidler and Heidler, *Encyclopedia of the American Civil War*, 3:1078.

32. Private Long confirmed Adair's detection of Southern sympathy for Union prisoners: "In a short time we received orders to be ready to start on the march. The next day while we were in this camp many citizens came out to see us, and some seemed to be very much affected at the sight they saw, and manifested much sympathy for us." He further speculated: "I have reason to believe that there was a strong union feeling in this town." Long, *Twelve Months in Andersonville*, 123–24.

all day long in water from half leg deep to waist deep & it was very cool to. I saw Maj Burks knock one of the prisoners off of a log with his saber. Just because he tried to keep out of the water. He then gave the guards orders to shoot any of the prisoners who should attempt to evade the water.[33] And by the time we went into camp we were numb with the cold. We camped in an old clearing where we had plenty of wood. And we soon had rousing fires made by rolling the big pitch logs together. We were then soon warm.

[December 22] Started early this morning and marched to Blue [Radium] Springs five miles from Albany. Where we encamped for the night and drew rations. We had plenty of good wood. And [illegible] as it is quite cool.

[December 23] Was called out last night at one o'clock. Only part of my hundred went out. The guards were stationed along on each side of the road, and as we marched out of the camp, the head of the column moved on while the guards for the rear stood fast. So we just march out of the guards. A great many tried to make their escape & were all brought back however with one exception. We got on board the cars at Albany and started for Andersonville, where we

33. Adair may very well have been referring to Pvt. W. B. Smith. In his postwar account, Smith recalls a remarkably similar incident. "The second day on this trip, about 10 A.M., we came to a creek, the water in which was about waist deep . . . the creek was not very wide, and across it two large trees were felled for the guards to walk over on, the prisoners being required to ford the stream. As I approached the stream and saw my comrades passing through the icy water . . . from the way my side and lung were paining me it seemed to me that if I should go in I should perish. I then foolishly broke ranks without asking permission of the guards and stepped upon the log between two of them as they were crossing over. It was with great difficulty that I balanced myself at all on the log, and could not walk fast enough to keep out of the way of the guard behind me. I had not taken more than four or five steps over the creek when the one immediately behind me, who was carrying his gun at a right shoulder shift, gave me a push with the butt of it in my back, and knocked me headlong into the water." See Smith, *On Wheels*, 264–65.

arrived about ten o'clock. And we were taken out and divided off in hundreds, until the roll of the hundred was taken so that there could be no flanking for rations. We were then taken into the prison and rations issued to us which consisted of one pint of burned rice. A heavy supper for men who had fasted all day.

CHAPTER 6

The Second Andersonville

ON DECEMBER 17, 1864, Gen. John Winder ordered the transfer of all prisoners from Thomasville to Andersonville.[1] Just four days earlier, Gen. William Sherman's men had captured Fort McAllister, a key defensive position some twelve miles south of Savannah, and begun preparing for a siege of the Georgia port city.[2] Thus, with communication to Savannah severed and the railroad cut between Savannah and Thomasville, the trajectory of Sherman's destructive march had forced yet another prisoner diaspora. This time the destination for the relocating prisoners was a known quantity, one with a horrific past; however, the prisoners soon discovered that Andersonville had developed a new identity.

The Andersonville story can be traced to late November 1863, when Capt. Sydney Winder received orders from J. W. Pegram, assistant adjutant general, to secure a site for a new prison facility in Georgia "in the neighborhood" of Americus or Fort Valley in the southwestern part of the state.[3] After a month-long search, Captain Winder selected a spot a mile and a half from Station No. 8 on the

---

1. *OR*, ser. II, vol. 7:1238.

2. For a detailed account of these actions, see Joseph T. Glatthaar, *The March to the Sea and Beyond: Sherman's Troops in the Savannah and Carolinas Campaign* (New York: New York Univ. Press, 1985).

3. *OR*, ser. II, vol. 6:558.

Georgia Southwestern Railroad near Andersonville, a community with a population of fewer than twenty people.[4]

The proposed prison site appeared to be a sound choice because the area "was heavily wooded with pine and oak, with the ground sloping down on both sides to a wide stream, a branch of Sweet Water Creek." Local opposition impeded the construction process from the start and forced Confederate authorities to impress slaves and materials in order to begin the job. The original plan called for the construction of a prison of barracks capable of holding 8,000–10,000 prisoners. However, deteriorating conditions in Richmond and supply shortages at key production and logistical points throughout the South forced Confederate officials to radically alter the original plan. "In desperation," as historian Lonnie Speer has noted, "the Confederate government ordered that a simple stockade—in effect just a corral, the cheapest, most economical form of confinement—be completed as soon as possible." On February 25, the first prisoners arrived and entered the prison grounds, although the stockade had not been completed.[5] The population grew steadily between February and May, with the four-month totals numbering 1,600, 4,603, 7,875, and 13,486, respectively. The average number of deaths per day for March, April, and May were 9, 19, and 23, respectively.[6]

For a variety of reasons, June marked a turning point in the tragic history of Andersonville Prison. On June 17, Gen. John Winder assumed command of the prison, replacing the first commandant, Col. Alexander W. Parsons. Winder, as the head of Confederate prisons in Georgia and Alabama, had ordered the appointment of Capt. Henry Wirz as commander of the interior of the prison. In mid-June, the two men faced an incredible task, as "there were nearly 22,300 prisoners in the pen that was built for only half as many,

4. Futch, *History of Andersonville Prison*, 3.

5. Speer, *Portals to Hell*, 259–60.

6. August C. Hamlin, *Martyria: or, Andersonville Prison* (Boston: Lee & Shepard, 1866), 245–46.

and already more than 2,600 had died."[7] Indeed, as historian William Marvel explains, an exponential rise in the prison population occurred within a matter of a few weeks: "The procession of new prisoners seemed never to end . . . nearly 1,200 entered the stockade on June 15, only somewhat fewer the next day, and over 400 more two days later. Another 877 entered the day after that, and 813 between June 21 and 24."[8] The overcrowding forced the Confederate officials to expand the prison compound by an additional ten acres to accommodate 10,000 prisoners. On July 1, "a ten-foot-wide hole was knocked into the existing wall, and 13,000 of the compound's 25,000 POWs were ordered to relocate within two hours or lose all their possessions."[9]

The expansion, however, did not solve the problem of overcrowding, because more prisoners continued to arrive in July and August. By the end of July, the population had reached 28,689, and by the end of August the number of prisoners at Andersonville had soared to 32,193. Every problem imaginable manifested itself during the sultry summer days of 1864. Poor sanitation, insufficient rations, and inadequate medical supplies and hospital facilities all contributed to the prison's high death toll. From July to the end of September, nearly 9,000 prisoners died at Andersonville, with August averaging ninety-nine and September eighty-nine deaths per day. An additional 2,245 prisoners died during October.[10]

Andersonville's reputation even haunted some Southerners, among them Eliza Frances Andrews. In January 1865, she and her sister fled Washington, Georgia, to escape an anticipated encounter with Sherman's armies. Destined for Albany, Georgia, the young women first stopped at Andersonville. On that January day, the Southern belle reflected, with obvious dismay, on the legacy of

---

7. Speer, *Portals to Hell*, 259–60. See Sanders, *While in the Hands of the Enemy*, 212.

8. Marvel, *Andersonville*, 91.

9. Speer, *Portals to Hell*, 261.

10. Hamlin, *Martyria*, 245–46.

the infamous prison: "I shuddered as I passed the place on the car, with its tall gibbet full of horrible suggestive-ness before the gate, and its seething mass of humanity inside, like a swam of blue flies crawling over a grave." Andrews feared Sherman's retributive wrath and believed that he "did not intend to leave so much as a blade of grass in South-West Georgia . . . [and] his soldiers have sworn that they will spare neither man, woman, nor child." But Yankee justice for the atrocities of Andersonville would have to wait until after the war. Meanwhile, Sherman would continue to march through Georgia and then on to South Carolina. Lyle Adair, who arrived a few weeks prior to Andrews's "visit," would await the end of the war in Andersonville.[11]

Andrews's lamentation referred to the "first" Andersonville. In September 1864, when William Sherman moved into Atlanta, Confederate authorities, fearing that Sherman might attempt to liberate the Union prisoners in southwest Georgia, ordered the depopulation of Andersonville. Prisoners exited in massive numbers, with many bound for either Savannah or Charleston. By October 1, the prison population at Andersonville had fallen to 8,218, and by the end of the month the total was down to 4,208.[12] During the months of November and December, the prison functioned more like a hospital, tending to the captives too sick to travel. In early December there were fewer than 1,500 men in Andersonville Prison, but by month's end the total was approaching 5,000.[13] Nevertheless, when Adair arrived at Andersonville two days before Christmas in 1864, the infamous prison was merely a shell of its former self.

Structurally, Andersonville was in decline. Illustrative of this was the dilapidated deadline that coursed in intervals throughout the camp. As for camp discipline at the "second" Andersonville, historian Ovid Futch opined that "on every hand were signs that the

11. Spencer Bidwell King Jr., ed., *The War-Time Journal of a Georgia Girl, 1864–1865* (Macon, Ga.: Ardivan Press, 1960), 64–65.

12. *OR*, ser. II, vol. 7:1082–83.

13. Marvel, *Andersonville*, 225.

Confederate sun was setting."[14] A truly bizarre incident occurred in mid-January 1865 when a woman, who reported her name as Ann Williams, arrived at Andersonville claiming to be a "refugee from Savannah." She immediately began fraternizing with the inmates, and after two days of her consorting, Captain Wirz discovered that this female guest had sexual relations "with at least seven" men "in barely twenty-four hours." According to one source, "Miss Williams denied she was a prostitute, claiming she took no money for her little trysts, but she carried a bundle of cash that may have hinted otherwise."[15]

Further evidence of the erosion of discipline transpired on the night of March 4, the occasion of Abraham Lincoln's second inaugural. During the night, Captain Wirz "heard the tooting of a brass band at a house near his family's quarters." Knowing "the only musicians at Camp Sumter were paroled Federal prisoners . . . Wirz shuddered to think what might be said if they were found so far from the prison at night." His investigation revealed that a captain in the 2nd Georgia reserves was transporting the musicians some "five miles into the country as entertainment for a party in honor of the colonel's wife, who presented the regiment with a flag." When Wirz confronted the captain, the Georgian disregarded the objection and claimed to have permission from an authority higher than Wirz. He then led "the Yankee musicians off into the night with their pinging, bonking instruments."[16]

Whereas the certainty of death taunted the prisoners of the first Andersonville, the incessant rumors of a parole or exchange mocked the prisoners of the second. To be sure, Union prisoners succumbed to overexposure, disease, and starvation during the latter incarnation. But deaths in the last month of 1864 and the first three months of 1865 numbered fewer than six per day.[17] Since July 1862,

14. Futch, *History of Andersonville Prison*, 114.
15. Marvel, *Andersonville*, 230.
16. Ibid., 233.
17. Hamlin, *Martyria*, 245.

the Dix-Hill Cartel had governed the prisoner exchange program by specifying the terms and equivalencies of exchange as well as locations for exchanges and paroles. Initially the system worked well, and Northern and Southern prisons "were almost empty by the fall of 1862." However, the frequency and regularity of paroles and exchanges deteriorated radically after President Lincoln announced the preliminary Emancipation Proclamation in late September 1862, an order he signed into law on January 1, 1863. Among other things, the proclamation provided for the enlistment of blacks as Union soldiers. Subsequently, the Confederate government refused to exchange white soldiers for black soldiers, which dramatically increased the prison populations in both the North and the South and stalled the exchange program.[18]

The Union also contributed to the halt of prisoner exchanges. In early 1863, the North held substantially more prisoners than the South. This prisoner gap widened as the war continued and affected the North's negotiating tactics. After General Ulysses S. Grant moved to the Eastern Theater and in effect assumed command of the federal war effort, he reasoned that the prisoner gap gave the North a decided military advantage and he therefore opposed wholesale exchanges. Grant was fully supported by Secretary of War Edwin Stanton and President Lincoln. As historian Charles W. Sanders Jr. has argued in compelling fashion, the tens of thousands of prisoners in Northern and Southern prison camps "would not have suffered and died as they did if the men who directed the prison systems . . . had followed their own regulations" and the requirements of "basic humanity." Ultimately, the inevitability of Southern defeat and "the unrelenting public pressure on the Lincoln administration to secure release of Union captives" convinced Grant to authorize regular exchanges in the spring of 1865.[19] Finally, on March 18, more than 900 prisoners departed Andersonville bound for the federal lines at Vicksburg. They

18. McPherson, *Ordeal by Fire*, 451.
19. Sanders, *While in the Hands of the Enemy*, 257, 315, 316, 274.

arrived nine days later.[20] In the coming weeks, train loads of prisoners left Andersonville on their quest for freedom. Unfortunately for Lyle G. Adair, he was among the last to pass through the gates. His seven-month prison ordeal provoked a variety of opinions and reactions, and none more haunting than the notion that he had been abandoned by his country and had been left to die in a Southern dungeon.

[December 24] Was extremely cold last night. We had but very little wood, so we had to go to bed to keep warm. We just leveled the earth which had been newly ploughed, and made our bed on that. We *suffered considerably* with the cold, during the night. Had roll call this morning. There were more prisoners came in today from Albany.

[December 25] Christmas Morning went to work and fixed up a shelter. About noon it commenced raining and rained all day. It was a very sorry Christmas to us who were in Camp Sumpter Prison.[21] We have drawn cooked rations altogether since we came here.

[December 26] We had a miserable night of it, rained all night and is still wet and damp this morning. There were more prisoners came in to day. They have not all reached here from Albany.[22] Some of the prisoners were found dead this morning. Two of which were

20. Marvel, *Andersonville*, 234.

21. The Christmas Day diary entry of Pvt. John A. Duff, Company A, 101st Pennsylvania Infantry, epitomizes the full range of emotions prisoners experienced on anniversaries and holidays: "Christmas. We had some fun in camp. One of the men disguised himself as a Reb officer and arrested some of the boys for trading with the guard. A merry Christmas at home I hope. But a dull one here. I should be thankful to God that he gave me my health in this prison life." John A. Duff Diary, Jan. 25, 1864, ADC.

22. The final prisoners from Thomasville did reach Andersonville on December 26. The prison population approached 5,000 with an additional 1,000 convalescing in the twenty-two buildings that made up the prison hospital ward. Security was tight; the security garrison increased to 1,400 with the guards who escorted the Thomasville prisoners. In fact, only two prisoners would reach freedom during the first month of 1865. Marvel, *Andersonville*, 228.

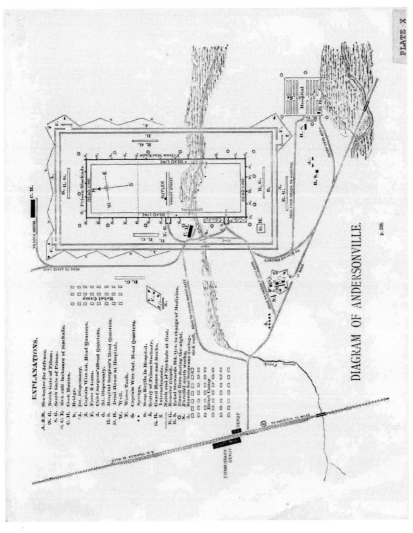

DIAGRAM OF ANDERSONVILLE.

p. 328.

A diagram of Andersonville Prison. Some have referred to the march from the train depot to the north gate as "800 paces to hell." Courtesy of Andersonville National Historic Site.

smothered to death by burrowing in the ground; the ground caving in on them in the night—while they were asleep.[23]

[December 27] We had to go to work and fill up the underground part of our house. We then made a wall of wood and banked the earth against it. I went down to the creek which runs through the prison and took a good wash. Rations short. Drew beans, beef, and corn bread.

[December 28] There was a very hard thunderstorm last night, rained very hard. We managed however to keep ourselves quite dry. Cleared off and is very cold to day. Rations very short. We only get three cords of bread to the hundred men. These cords were twenty inches long by 12 inches wide and one and a half inches thick. And three of these cords constituted one day's rations for one hundred men.[24]

23. Cpl. George Marion Shearer, Company E, 17th Iowa Infantry, arrived at Andersonville on December 24, 1864, the day after Adair. His diary confirms the two suffocations and two additional deaths. Shearer estimated that the prison population at that time was 3,500. George Marion Shearer Diary, Dec. 26, 1864, ADC. Pvt. M. J. Umsted added additional commentary and suggested the tunneling was not an attempt to escape: "Yesterday quite a number of men tunneled into the side of a hill in the stockade so as to shelter themselves from the cold and wet. Once during the night one of the caves fell in killing 4 men." Umsted Diary, Dec. 26, 1864. Pvt. William Lightcap explained that as the torrential rains rolled down the prison terrain "four others [prisoners] went about twenty feet from us and started their hole higher up and succeeded in getting a good shelter, and there they remained until they were dug out the next morning, for during the night the bank cracked a few feet back and turned over. The poor fellows were smothered and crushed, a pitiful sight to see, faces black and blue and blood oozing from mouth, nose and ears." Lightcap, *The Horrors of Southern Prisons*, 70. In his investigation of the deaths, historian William Marvel discovered that two skeletons were unearthed at Andersonville on April 28, 1899. He concluded that "no contemporary source mentions the Christmas victims being exhumed at all, and doubts expressed . . . about a third body inside the collapsed borrow further suggest the remains were not immediately recovered—and that would explain the lack of documentation in the hospital register." Marvel, *Andersonville*, 228, 301n41.

24. Private Umsted also complained of the small rations: "Quite exciting times today as the Rebs are trying to starve us to death. Our rations heretofore have been very small but now they are cut down again to ¾ pound of heavy coarse corn bread, 2 oz. of beef and 1 pint of cooked beans for a days ration. Men are suffering very much from the effect of it." Umsted Diary, Dec. 28, 1864.

This photo was taken in August 1864 from a sentry box, looking northeast. The deadline is visible in the right foreground. Courtesy of Andersonville National Historic Site.

[December 29] Turned very cold last night. This morning they are laying out the camp in streets so that each hundred and division may be in its places and come in position as they are numbered commencing with the first division at the prison gate. The main st runs east & west. Our Co. is on hundred[, which] runs North & South.

[December 30] Had to move our camp to the grounds assigned us for camping. We are in the Fourth hundred 2nd Div in the prison. We got pretty well fixed up to day. It is quite warm. Wilson & Hagerty were appointed on the police and had to move to Police Head-Quarters today.

[December 31] Came up a hard storm during the night, rained very hard & this morning is very cold again and remained cold all day.[25] New Year's Eve and shall we ever spend another New Year's Eve in the enjoyment of home & friends or is this the last one we are to be permitted to spend on Earth? God only knows. But we shall live in *hope* knowing that let what will be our fate, it is all for the best. And this ends the (to me) the eventful year of 1864.

January 1st 1865
Thus a New Year dawns up us; here in this most loathsome places "Andersonville Prison." The sergeants of each hundred, have been furnished a copy of the rules and regulations of the prison (which I here copy).

25. In late December, the Confederates attempted to rebuild the deadline. However, the frigid winter temperatures even coaxed the guards to leave their sentry boxes in search of camp fires on the prison grounds. The cover of darkness allowed the suffering prisoners "to pilfer" boards or cross the line in search of kindling. On New Year's Eve night of 1864, a "suspicious guard" caught Christian Konrad attempting to abscond with a board from the deadline and "dropped the frail immigrant with a bullet through the head." The death of one prisoner did not deter the survivors. "A few nights later," as Marvel writes, "the new deadline came down, covertly sacrificed for a little heat. Day after the day, the bored, hungry, raggedly clad Federals hovered over snapping, fist-sized fires, toasting their bellies while their backs rippled with goose bumps." Marvel, *Andersonville*, 228–29.

Rules and Regulations of the Prison

 I. There will be two daily Roll Calls at the Prison, one at eight o'clock a.m. and one at four o'clock p.m.

 II. The prisoners are divided into detachments of one hundred men each, five detachments constitutes a Division.

 III. Each division must occupy the ground assigned them for encampment, no huts or tents must be erected outside of the camping grounds.

 IV. Each detachment must elect a sergeant; the five sergeants of the division will appoint one of their number to draw rations for the whole division.

 V. The sergeants are responsible for the cleanliness of their encampment. They will each day make a detail from among their men for policing the camp throughout; any man refusing to do police duty will be punished by the sergts by balling him the rest of the day.

 VI. No rations will be issued to any division unless all the men are present at roll call. The sergeants in charge of the detachment must report every absentee. If he fails to do so and it turns out that the missing man has escaped, he will be put in close confinement until the missing man is recaptured.

 VII. The sergeant of a detachment will report all those sick in his detachment and will carry them after roll call at eight o'clock a.m. in the morning, to the receiving hospital. After examination by the surgeon in charge he will leave those who are admitted and carry the others back. He will at the same time take charge of those belonging to his division who may be discharged from the hospital.

 VIII. The prisoners have the privilege to write twice a week. No letter must be over one page in length and must contain nothing but private matters.

 IX. And prisoner has a right to ask for an interview with the commanding officer of the prison by applying to the sergeant of the gate between the hours of ten and eleven a.m.

x. The sergeants of detachments and divisions must report to the commandant of the prison any short-coming of rations.

xi. No prisoner must cross the dead line, nor speak to any sentinel on post nor attempt to buy or sell anything to a sentinel. The sentinel having orders to fire on any one crossing the dead line or attempting to speak to or trade with them.

xii. It is the duty of the detachment sergeants to carry any men who should die in quarters immediately to the receiving hospital. Giving the hospital clerk the name, rank, company, regiment, and state of division.

xiii. To prevent stealing in camp the prisoners have a right to elect a chief of police who will select as many men as he may deem necessary to assist him. He and the sergeants of the divisions have a right to punish any man who is detected stealing. The punishment shall be shaving of one half the head and a number of lashes not exceeding fifty. And these were the orders to which we the prisoners of Andersonville were subject.

[January 12] Nothing of any importance has occurred during the past few days; except that it has been very cold. It is reported by some of the guards that Kilpatrick has taken Macon. One of the guards told me yesterday that we would likely be moved from here soon as some of the Yankee raiders were around. Got out yesterday for wood.[26] Got good rations in comparison to what we usually get. The police have shut down on men selling their rations.[27] They do not allow the men to sell any thing we draw nor to have such things on their

26. Cpl. George Shearer recalled that "100 men from each division" were permitted to leave camp on January 11 to collect wood. Shearer Diary, Jan. 11, 1865.

27. Corporal Shearer made reference to the currency exchange rate inside the prison: "Confederate money has decreased in value within the last few days. It can be bought 8 & 10 for one in greenback." Shearer Diary, Jan. 14, 1865.

stands. If they do keep such things, they will be confiscated by the police.[28] Went out for fire wood again today in jacks[?] He can go or send a man if he pleases.

[January 15] Has been very pleasant but cool for the past two days. Went out yesterday for wood. Looked like rain all day yesterday. But has cleared off and is now very cold. Last night we had a very heavy frost. Drew soap yesterday, and all the black and dirty men who would not wash themselves, were taken to the creek by the police and made to wash. It is reported that we are to be taken to Memphis in a few days for exchange. Oh! that this might prove to be true! Something more than mere rumor. But we have been disappointed so frequently, we hardly dare to live in hopes of anything more.

[January 18] On the night of the 15th I dreamed of returning home. Oh! what would I not give to hear from home ones more. Yesterday and day before was very cold. But today is quite warm & pleasant. Have been quite unwell all day. Jack McEwen is quite sick also. One of the prisoners made his escape last night and some who made their escape from Thomasville and had got nearly to our lines were recaptured and brought in yesterday. They report an exchange in hand. I sincerely hope this may be true. We naturally feel like exclaiming How long! Oh Lord! How long are we thus to suffer the penalty of being our country's defenders.

[January 21] It rained steady all the night of the 20th. And has been raining incessantly ever since. Today we borrowed a pack of cards and played poker, until rations came in. It is very cold & disagreeable. And

28. The police presence did not thwart the wheeling and dealing of Pvt. Asberry Stephen of Company H, 116th OVI. From January 13 to 15, Smith made numerous notations in his diary of his trading activities, including the "$2 in Confed" that he earned on January 13 and the "15 cts" he made on January 15. In fact, on January 15 he wrote that after roll call he was "all over and on the make again" searching for "grub." Oscar F. Curtis, ed., *The Civil War Diary of Asberry C. Stephen* (Bloomington, Ind.: Monroe County Historical Society, 1973), 30.

very loathsome without anything to read; or any way to pass the time. Everyday brings the same round of monotony. No news. No change. But sleep! sleep!! sleep!!! from twelve to fourteen hours out of every twenty four. Since we came here there have been some changes in our mess. It is now composed of seven in number. John McEwen (or Jack for short) A Scotchman by birth and an old sailor, though a very wicked man he is one of the most cleaver, kind hearted and accommodating men I ever met. He is a member of the Thirty-fifth New Jersey Infantry. Next came Chas Monroe of the 111th Illinois Infantry (or Father as we called him for short). Then came John Gibson of the 43rd Ohio Infantry (or Dock for short). Next Alex McWhorter of the 101st Pa Infantry. Next Allen Miller of the 24th New York Cavalry. Next [William H.] Hafer of the 2nd Ohio Cavalry and last came P[eter]. W. Duffield of the [Company C] 81st Ohio Infantry (or grand father as they called him). This composed our mess and a more jovial and contented set of men I do not suppose could be found in the prison. Even playing pranks at each other's expense.

[January 24] On the 22nd It rained all day and was very disagreeable. Rations came in very early this morning. The Rebel Recruiting Officers came in recruiting but did not take any with them.[29] On the 23rd got out for wood in the morning. The recruiting officers came in again to day for recruits.[30] The prisoners are just flocking to enlist,[31] in order to escape from the prison.[32] Its very cold and

29. The group was led by Lt. Col. J. G. O'Neil of the 10th Tennessee Infantry. The previous fall O'Neil had recruited some 250 Galvanized Rebels from Camp Lawton near Millen, Georgia. Marvel, *Andersonville*, 223, 231.

30. George Shearer estimated that 150 prisoners took the oath. Shearer Diary, Jan. 23, 1865. Pvt. Asberry Stephen indicated "some 60" went out on Sunday, January 22. The next day he noted, "Rain comes down. And a lot going out." Curtis, *The Civil War Diary of Asberry C. Stephen*, 31.

31. More than twenty-five years after his release, Pvt. W. B. Smith painted a somewhat different picture of the men and numbers of men who took "the oath of allegiance to the Confederate government": "I remember but three or four whom I saw go out . . . and they were under guard, or I believe they would have been lynched by their comrades . . . no doubt some who took this oath did so with the view of making escape to our lines after reaching the front." Smith, *On Wheels*, 277.

32. Pvt. John A. Duff and Sgt. John C. Ely, Company C, 115th OVI, estimated, respectively, that "150 or more" and "some 200" prisoners took the oath. Pvt. M. J.

disagreeable. Yesterday evening, five hundred more prisoners came in. They were captured by [John B.] Hood in Tenn. They report Hood badly used up and returning for Richmond. Joe Johnston is in command of the army. One hundred and forty prisoners enlisted & went out to day.[33]

[January 25] Its very cold and disagreeable, and we have but very little wood to make fires to keep us warm. We have to carry all the wood we get from one and a half to two miles on our shoulders and it only comes our regular turns about once in every fourteen days. And at that once going out, we have to carry enough to do us that long. It is just four months today since I was captured.[34]

[January 26] Still very cold.[35] We went to work and tried to raise meal enough to make us a pot of mush. Sold our rations of molasses for thirty cents and as meal sells for fifteen cents per quart we were enabled to get two quarts of meal which we were saving until we can get two more quarts.

[January 27] The rebels were in recruiting again to day. The have got about three hundred recruits in all from the prison. Several prisoners froze to death last night. One of the prisoners who was

---

Umsted recorded: "I believe for the best I can learn they recruited and enlisted 168." Duff Diary, Jan. 23, 1865; John C. Ely Diary, Jan. 24, 1865, ADC; Umsted Diary, Jan. 23, 1865.

33. Corporal Shearer recorded that "about 150 union Prisoners [went] into the rebel service. 500 Prisoners brought here from Meredian Miss." Shearer Diary, Jan. 23, 1865. In his postwar prison reminiscence, Pvt. William Lightcap's recollections of the Galvanized Rebels appeared more sympathetic in comparison to the diarists' accounts. Lightcap stated that the Confederate offer "instead of temping us it made us wrathy." He did concede regrettably: "There were a few who weakened and went out. I do not believe any of them lost their love for the old flag, but as they expressed it, they did so to save their lives. They did not believe they could live through it to the end in there." They exited, Lightcap concluded, "to forever be disgraced." Lightcap, *The Horrors of Southern Prisons*, 71.

34. An additional forty-two Galvanized Rebels joined O'Neil two days after the first visit. Marvel, *Andersonville*, 231.

35. Pvt. John Duff, who at the time had been a prisoner for more than nine months, noted: "The coldest day I have felt since a prisoner." Duff Diary, Jan. 26, 1865.

froze, was carried out for dead and laid inside the dead line at the gate. When the sun shone on him awhile some of the other prisoners, who were at the gate discovered signs of returning life and got permission and removed him to a tent where they bathed him and worked with him until they were rewarded by the knowledge that they had been instrumental in saving the life of one fellow man. "Or rather saving one man from a living grave."

[January 28] Still very cold and windy. Rations very slow about coming in and *very small* when they get in.[36]

[January 29] It is just three months today since we left Cahaba Prison. It is much more pleasant today as it has moderated and is quite warm. The rebel papers report that President Lincoln has issued another proclamation offering rebels terms upon which to return to the Union. We sincerely hope that we may not have much longer to remain in prison.

[January 30] There is a strong talk of peace in the rebel papers. The weather is very pleasant, sun shining and warm. It is just one year to day since I was last mustered into service for three years.

[January 31] It is very pleasant and warm today. The papers report that peace commissioners have been sent to Washington to try and negotiate peace. I sincerely hope that they may succeed in making an honorable peace. Otherwise I will remain in prison in preference to having any thing done for our release which will bring disgrace upon the union arms.

[February 1] There were four of the old Cahaba prisoners came in today from Macon, Ga. Fryburger[?] (one of my regt) was one of the

36. Conversely, Pvt. Asberry Stephen noted with pleasure the success of trading "molasses for meat and had quite a large meal." Curtis, *The Civil War Diary of Asberry C. Stephen,* 32.

number.[37] He tells me that all the officers and sutlers[38] of our regt were released on parole and sent to our lines after they had been in prison about one month.

[February 2] It is cloudy and damp today. We had our feast this evening. After eating all the rations we drew for today we were still almost perishing with hunger. I managed to get two quarts of beans which we cooked until they would mash up & then mixing them with the two quarts of meal we had, which we baked in a dutch oven we had on hand. And four of us in number consumed all of this after eating all our rations, and were still hungry. So from this you may judge of the size of our rations.

[February 3] Is raining this morning. We had not even wood enough to keep us warm. So we had to cover up in bed to keep warm until rations came in. The rebel paper stated that the question of a general exchange would soon be decided.[39]

[February 4] Was cool & cloudy all day. Got out and got plenty of wood to day but got very small rations. Have had a very sore hand but it is much better today.[40]

37. Sgt. John Ely noted that "155 prisoners" came in from Macon on that day. Ely Diary, Feb. 1, 1865.

38. Sutlers were civilian merchants with military authorization to sell goods to individual troops or to a post. For more on sutlers and their activities, see Heidler and Heidler, Encyclopedia of the American Civil War, 4:1910–11.

39. On February 2, 1865, Gen. Ulysses S. Grant decided to begin a carefully controlled prisoner exchange program. The goal was to exchange approximately 3,000 prisoners per week, "but in order to ensure that no advantage accrued to southern arms, Grant specified that only invalids who had been recruited from areas of the South already under Union control were to be sent through the lines." Historian Charles Sanders has concluded that "the exchanges authorized by Grant in the spring of 1865 were initiated to ease the unrelenting public pressure on the Lincoln administration to secure release of Union captives." Sanders, While in the Hands of the Enemy, 274–75.

40. The sore hand could have been related to the wood chopping duties. Pvt. John Duff "blistered" his hand after a day of chopping wood around the same time as Adair's injury. Duff Diary, Feb. 8, 1865.

This photo was taken in August 1864 during the issuing of rations. At the time there were approximately 33,000 prisoners at Andersonville, significantly more than the 5,000 there during Adair's stay. Courtesy of Andersonville National Historic Site.

[February 5] Sabbath day has been cool & cloudy all day. Does not seem much like the Sabbath today. Staid in quarters all day. Drew very small rations this eve. Nothing new in regard to exchange hope there will be soon.

[February 6] Was cool and cloudy this morn. Went out for wood again today.[41] Is very cold & raw. We got plenty of wood. It has been raining nearly all day!

[February 7] Still wet and raining. The old Capt (Wirtz) was in today. Threatened to stop our rations in the whole camp because a few of the prisoners hollered at and made fun of him.[42]

[February 8] Very cold & windy today. I went out for wood came very near perishing with the cold for the wind was blowing very cold and very hard from the North.[43]

[February 9] Went through the grave yard where the martyred Union dead are buried. It is a sight from which the stoutest heart would quail to see the graves of some fourteen thousand Union men whose bodies lie molding here beneath the Georgia sand martyred for Union and Liberty.

41. Pvt. W. B. Smith claimed that "not oftener than every twenty or twenty-five days during that winter [1865] each prisoner was permitted to go out, under guard, to carry in wood, going about a quarter mile for it. It was astonishing to see the great logs brought in by some of the boys who looked as if they could scarcely stand on their feet." Smith, *On Wheels*, 279–80.

42. A week earlier, Private Umsted made a similar comment: "No news today only it is reported that Capt. Wirz Commanding Officer of this prison has said that he is going to starve every Yank in it—to take the oath of allegiance to the C.S.G. and I think he is doing it for we do not get enough rations for one meal per day and I think that is putting us on short rations." Umsted Diary, Jan. 28, 1865.

43. Umsted described that day as "quite a blustery day, cold, and cloudy." He added, "Snowed some this evening. I never expected to see it snow down here in Georgia." Umsted Diary, Feb. 7, 1865.

This photo, taken in August 1864, captures prisoners burying the dead in six-foot-wide trenches. The death tolls for the summer months of 1864 were 1,738 in July, 3,081 in August, and 2,678 in September. Nearly 13,000 prisoners died at Andersonville. Their identity was preserved due, in large measure, to the work of Clara Barton and Dorence Atwater during the summer of 1865. Courtesy of Andersonville National Historic Site.

[February 10] Is very cold and windy today. We had to do with but very little wood as [but] some of us got out for wood. There is good news from Sherman's army. It is reported that he has cut off communications with Richmond.

[February 11] Got out for wood this morning. The Peace Commission accomplished nothing.[44] The word now is fight on till death. Or till the rebels lay down their arms in submission to the Union authorities.

[February 12] The Sabbath day. It is a bright & beautiful day. One of my mess [mates] got out for wood today. Weather cool. John Thompson, Jack and I, all got shaved today for the first time since our capture. My hair and beard got to coming out so I concluded have it off.

[February 13] Most of us got out for wood today. Weather quite cool. The rebels sent in the cooks from the cook house today. They are going to issue us raw rations hereafter.

[February 14] Is raining this morning, continued raining all day. This evening drew raw rations for the first time. Good news in the papers Congress has taken the exchange in hand. Hope something may be done to release us from prison.[45]

44. On February 3, 1865, Confederate vice president Alexander Stephens headed a three-man Southern peace delegation that met with Union leaders on President Lincoln's yacht, the *River Queen*, near Fort Monroe in Virginia. At the Hampton Roads Conference, Stephens proposed an armistice and "a cooling-off period and possible joint action against the French in Mexico." The French had helped to install Maximilian I as emperor of Mexico. Lincoln refused to consider any plan that did not include reunion and the emancipation of slaves, conditions the Confederacy would not accept, and the conference ended after just four hours. Near the end of the meeting, Stephens "asked Lincoln about a prisoners exchange; the president referred him to Grant. As they rose to leave, Lincoln asked Stephens if there was anything else he could do." Stephens informed the president that his nephew, John A. Stephens, had been captured during the fall of Port Hudson during the summer of 1863 and was being held at Johnson's Island in Lake Erie. Lincoln promised to investigate. Thomas E. Schott, *Alexander Stephen: A Biography* (Baton Rouge: Louisiana State Univ. Press, 1988), 473–47.

45. Private Umsted had a slightly different perspective on the motives of the national legislature: "Congress has taken up the question (of the treatment of prisoners) in

[February 15] Was very misty & foggy this morning. But has cleared off and is quite pleasant this evening. We drew our rations early today.

[February 16] I sprained my shoulder this morning, suffered greatly from it. But is now some better. Is very pleasant today. There is a raid reported in motion for this place for the release of the prisoners.

[February 17] Drew our rations early this morning. Is very pleasant with the exception that it is very muddy. Was very windy this evening the wind blowing extremely hard. No news today.

[February 18] Is very pleasant some fifty more prisoners came in today. They were captured by Hood. They are the most destitute looking set of men I ever saw.[46] News to day of a general exchange being on foot. Our dying hopes are raised again and we feel in hopes that something may be in store for us in the future better than we anticipate. Oh Liberty! How I long to stand again beneath the folds of the stars and stripes.

[February 19] Went to the hospital for Munson who is sick. No news today. Weather warm & pleasant.

---

hand and that they have issued retaliatory orders and that rebel prisoners held in the north shall be treated the same as those in the south." Umsted Diary, Feb. 14, 1865. In late January 1865, the U.S. Senate once again debated the issue that called for retaliatory retribution against Confederate prisoners of war in response to mistreatment of Union prisoners in Southern camps. Although there were several retaliation backers, most notably Benjamin Wade of Ohio, who even sponsored a measure that would have removed Union prison officials who failed to implement retaliation policies, the final resolution that passed the Senate lacked any "in-kind retaliation" provisions. The debate at the time was moot, since prisoner exchanges had been well under way since early February. See Bruce Tap, *Over Lincoln's Shoulder: The Committee on the Conduct of the War* (Lawrence: Univ. Press of Kansas, 1998), 208.

46. On this date, Cpl. George Shearer recorded that 700 prisoners entered Andersonville from the "west"; he agreed with Adair that the men "look hard and care-worn." Sgt. John Ely estimated that "some 800 prisoners" arrived that day, "the sick left at Meridian, captured of Hood." Shearer Diary, Feb. 18, 1865; Ely Diary, Feb. 18, 1865.

[February 20] Miller & I went out for wood. Both together brought in a large stick of wood. Did some washing today and in the evening went to the creek and took a good bath as the Rebels issued us plenty of soap this morning.

[February 21] Was very cloudy this morning and cool. But is clearing off quite pleasant.

[February 22] Weather warm and pleasant. Drew rations early. More news of the exchange in today's paper. General Grant is now to push it forward as speedily as possible.

[February 23] Rained nearly all night. It is quite cool today. We took a vote today as to whether we should have barracks or not.[47] As the rebels are getting very good and are building sheds for us.[48] My division voted no barracks.[49]

47. Pvt. William Lightcap also thought the improvement a bit contrived. "During the later part of February, the Rebs, realizing that the war was fast drawing to a close and believing that the prisons would soon be inspected by Federal officials, began to prepare for as good a showing as possible. They . . . erected sheds as fast as possible, similar to northern farmers' hay sheds. A long roof supported about fifteen feet in the air on poles. They were not much good for shelters for the roofs were too high and not boarded upon the sides or ends . . . a cowardly piece of deception that I trust did not deceive our officials." Lightcap, *The Horrors of Southern Prisons*, 75–76.

48. Sgt. J. B. Vawter, Company C, 4th Kentucky Mounted Infantry, interpreted the barracks construction in a slightly different manner than Lightcap did: "During the month of February the rebels . . . had three sheds erected. These sheds were about twenty-five feet wide, by one hundred and fifty long; about five feet high at the eaves, and ten or twelve feet high in the center—roofed with boards, and left open on all sides. They were designed for a shelter for those who had no blankets or tents of any kind; and during a hard rain one thousand men would crowd under each shed. When it was not raining most of the men preferred to remain outside, on account of the vermin—especially fleas—which were so much worse in the dry sand under these roofs than in other parts of the prison. In the different narratives of Andersonville prison life, I have never seen any account of building of these sheds; but I am glad to give to the notorious Winder and Wirtz credit for this much humanity. Perhaps the reader thinks it is no great thing to build such sheds. True. And yet they were a blessing to a number of wretched prisoners who were almost naked, and had there been more of them built in the fall, they would have saved many lives. J. B. Vawter, *Prison Life in Dixie: A Short History of the Inhuman and Barbarous Treatment of Our Soldiers by Rebel Authorities* (Chicago: Central Book Concern, 1918), 165–66.

49. It is unlikely that Sgt. John Ely, who arrived at Andersonville a month later,

[February 24] Was raining this morning and continued raining all day. Rations came in very early.

[February 25] Is raining still this morning and quite cool. It is just five months to day since I was taken prisoner. I have the scurvy very bad in my mouth.[50] Is very hard to work to get any thing for it here.

[February 26] Rained very hard last night, but is clear and pleasant to day. It looks very much like Spring. I am much better off [with my] scurvy today. No more news from the outside. This is the Sabbath day. Yet how unlike the holy Sabbath to us.

[February 27] Turned very cool toward morning. Is still cool & cloudy today. The news looks favorable for us to be exchanged soon. Col. O'Neil comes in again to recruit for the Tenth Tenn Rebel Regt.

[February 28] Col. O'Neil came in again to day for recruits. Got quite a number from among the prisoners.[51] Alex McWhorter, one of my mess mates went out and took the oath to support the Confederacy. This is the last day of the month. The papers stated today that Charleston, SC was in the hands of the Union army. I came across verses composed by A. J. Hyatt of Co. K 118th Pa volls while dying at the hospital outside the stockade.[52] I herewith copy

---

was in the same division as Adair. Nevertheless, Ely recorded that "division sergeants sent communication to Capt. Wirtz relative to changing quarters, refused." Ely Diary, Feb. 23, 1865.

50. Scurvy is a disease caused by malnutrition, specifically the lack of vitamin C. The first symptoms include listlessness and fatigue, then swollen and bleeding gums and the loosening of teeth. Contemporary doctors also observed that scurvy increased bleeding from open wounds. "Civil War physicians blamed the extremely high fatality rates in prisons, particularly at Andersonville, on the prisoners' malnutrition and, specifically, on scurvy." Alfred Jay Bollet, *Civil War Medicine: Challenges and Triumphs* (Tucson, Ariz.: Galen Press, 2002), 347, 332.

51. Pvt. John Duff set the number of Galvanized Rebels at "about 125." Duff Diary, Feb. 28, 1865.

52. The origins and authorship of "They Have Left Us Here to Die" remain shrouded in mystery. Adair attributed the poem to a Pennsylvania private by the name of A. J. Hyatt (or possibly H. J. Hyatt), Company K, 118th Pennsylvania Volunteer Infantry.

the verses which express the sentiments of the poor suffering and dying prisoners of Andersonville.

1st

When our country called for me we came from forge and store
and mill.
From workshop, farm and factory the broken ranks to fill;
We left our quite happy homes, and one we loved so well;
To vanquish all the Union foes, or fall where others fell;
Now in a prison drear we languish and it is our constant cry;
Oh! Ye who yet can save us, will you leave us here to die?

2nd

The voices of slander tells you that our hearts are weak with fear.
That all or nearly all of us were captured in the rear;
The scars upon our bodies from musket ball and shell;
The missing legs and shattered arms a true tale will tell;
We have tried to do our duty in the sight of God on high;
Oh! Ye who yet can save us, will you leave us here to die?

In this instance, the script in Adair's diary is difficult to decipher. However, Samuel P. Bates's record of Pennsylvania soldiers who served in the Civil War does not list an A. J. or H. J. Hyatt; the closest match is James W. Hyatt of Company H of the 118th. The Andersonville prisoner database confirms that Pvt. James W. Hyatt died on December 3, 1864 (roughly three weeks before Adair arrived), of diarrhea and is buried in grave number 12215. Adair, however, was not the only prisoner to reference the poem. Pvt. Calvin W. Diggs, 84th Indiana Volunteer Infantry, who at various times was a prisoner at Libby and Danville prisons in Virginia and at Millen and Andersonville prisons in Georgia, made an effort to preserve the poem after his release in the spring of 1865. At the parole center in Annapolis, Maryland, Diggs copied the poem onto a sheet of U.S. Sanitary Commission stationery. He made very few notations about the poem and attributed it to a T. J. Wyet of a Pennsylvania unit. Again Bates's record of Pennsylvania soldiers who served in the Civil War does not list a T. J Wyet, nor does the Andersonville prisoner database. Pvt. William Lightcap attributed the poem to an unnamed "scholastic comrade." Another prisoner copied the poem on the "margin of a Macon newspaper, and Lightcap obtained a copy after the war. Prior to the publication of his prison memoir, Lightcap lost the poem. However, he reproduced three of the four stanzas in his book, omitting stanza three. See Lightcap, *The Horrors of Southern Prisons*, 78. More than fifty years after the war was over, Alson H. L. Blake, a former corporal in Company F, 9th Vermont Volunteers, added more

3rd

Then are hearts with hopes still beating in our pleasant Northern
homes

Waiting; waiting; for the footstep that may never more return;

In Southern prisons pining; meager; tattered; pale and gaunt;

Growing weaker; weaker; daily from pinching cold and want;

Their brothers; sons; and husbands; poor and helpless captured be;

Oh! Ye who yet can save us, will you leave us here to die?

4th

Just out our prison gate there is a grave yard near at hand;

Where lie twelve thousand Union men beneath the Georgia sand;

Scores and scores we lay beside them as day succeeds each day;

And this it will be ever until they all shall pass away;

And the last can say when dying with upturned and glazing eye;

Both love and faith are dead at home, they have left us here to die.

[March 1] March came in raining and wet. Rained all night & is still
raining today. We drew meal today in place of beans got about one
quart to the man.

[March 2] Rained all night and is still raining this morning. I went
out for wood this morning. Has cleared off this morning and had

---

confusion to the origin and authorship of the poem. After brief confinements at the
Confederate prison camps in Wilmington and Salisbury, N.C., Blake arrived at Andersonville on May 31, 1864, where he remained until the end of the war. In a reunion
speech in Iowa before former prisoners, Blake implied that he authored the poem.
The onetime hospital steward recalled his days at Andersonville, where he observed
death and suffering in unbelievable proportions. To commemorate and preserve the
experience, Blake stated, "I have composed a few verses I will read if it will not weary
your patience"; he then recited "Will You Leave Us Here to Die." It is highly unlikely
that the former Vermont corporal authored the poem, because at least two independent sources attribute the poem to the yet-to-be-identified Pennsylvania soldier and
the reunion speech is the first time that Blake's name is linked to the poem. Samuel
P. Bates, *History of Pennsylvania Volunteers, 1861–1865,* 5 vols. (Harrisburg, Pa.: B.
Singerly State Printer, 1869–71), 3:1335; Calvin Diggs Papers, ANHS; Alson H. L. Blake
Papers, ANHS.

the appearance of being pleasant weather for a while. There is good news in the paper today on exchange.

[March 3] Opened up bright and clear this morning. There was some new prisoners came in last night. They belong to Sherman's army. And were captured in South Carolina. They say the exchange is all right.[53]

[March 4] This is the day of President Lincoln's inauguration. We have now had almost four years of war and bloodshed. We had a very hard rain storm this morning and it is still cloudy and damp.

[March 5] I was quite unwell all night with a severe headache and bad cold, which made me very restless. Today is clear and cool. This is the Sabbath day and yet how little like the Sabbath to us who are in prison.

[March 9] It has been wet and very rainy all day. Our tent leaks very bad. So that we have a damp time of it when it rains. More good news came in today in regard to the exchange. It is reported that the Cahaba prisoners have all been exchanged.

[March 10] Turned very cold last night. This morning it is cold and windy. Went out for wood to day passed through the grave yard and saw the graves of the Raiders who were hung on 6th of July 1864.[54]

53. Ely confirmed the arrival of 100 prisoners from Sherman's army; Umsted set the number at 105. Ely Diary, Mar. 2, 1865; Umsted Diary, Mar. 2, 1865.

54. The Andersonville Raiders were a group of Union prisoners who attacked and bullied their fellow inmates during the summer of 1864. More than just a handful of ruffians, the Raiders was a well-organized and well-managed group of 400–500 bandits. They beat, robbed, terrorized, and, in some cases, killed their comrades. In late June, a would-be victim resisted their attempts to steal his watch, and this inspired prisoners to fight back. Directly or indirectly related to this incident, Captain Wirz became concerned with the mayhem and allowed the prison inmates to conduct a judicial proceeding against the leaders of the Raiders. They were convicted of murder by their fellow prisoners and sentenced to die. On July 11, A. Nunn, Charles Curtis, John Sarsfield, Patrick Delaney, William Collins, and Cary Sullivan were hanged. Futch, *History of Andersonville*, 63–74.

[March 11] Was very cold last night. There is a report in circulation to day that the exchange will commence from this prison next week. It is very cool & windy to day.

[March 12] Sabbath morning. Cool but clear & pleasant. Captain Wirtz sent in word that we would all be exchanged inside of two weeks at the farthest.

[March 13] Very pleasant this morning. Was no wood squad sent out until after the train came in, as they were expecting orders for some of us to leave. But no orders came for us today. It has been extremely warm and sultry today.

[March 14] Was very warm today. This evening it commenced raining. The guards report that they are expecting orders everyday for some of us to leave here for exchange or parole.

[March 15] It rained nearly all night and is still raining this morning. We drew pork yesterday evening and again today. None have left here yet. The trains are running very busy for the past few days.

[March 16] Late yesterday even Col. [George C.] Gibbs[55] came into the prison & told us we were going to be exchanged but that it might be one month before all of us could get out. It has been very stormy today but has cleared off cool and windy.

[March 17] Just eleven years ago today, father departed this life. I was then in my eleventh year. The fleas bothered us so last night that we could not sleep. I got up and made a little fire, and sat by it and the fleas got on my feet just as fast as I could kill them. Thus I put in the

55. When Gen. John Winder moved his headquarters from Andersonville to Camp Lawton in October 1864, he appointed Col. George C. Gibbs as commander of Camp Sumter, although Captain Wirz was in charge of the prison and prisoners. Ibid., 113.

time, till morning. This morning took everything out of the tent and set the boughs on fire to kill the fleas. Then I took and boiled our blankets. Today is very warm and pleasant. The peach and plum trees are out in full bloom. Everything begins to look like Spring.

[March 18] It was quite cool last night. But is warm and very sultry today. They took out the sick today for exchange. They took one thousand. So the break is made.[56] The excitement runs high. Our hopes are buoyant, our spirits are raised high. God grant that they may not be just as suddenly dashed to the ground.

[March 19] Sunday morning. It was very cold last night but has been very warm today. Rebels came in to day for men to go out on parole to work.[57] They said there was only a special exchange for those who were already gone. And that no more of us were to be taken out.

[March 20] It is very pleasant and very warm today. Every one looks anxiously forward to the morn hoping, anxiously waiting for more prisoners to get out for exchanges, each one anxiously waiting for his turn to come.

[March 21] Clouded up late yesterday evening and last night rained hard and steady nearly all night, and on until noon today. We are still anxiously, waiting, watching, for the train to take more prisoners away.

56. William Marvel places the number at "more than nine hundred." Those released "were patients from the hospital; each side tried now to unburden itself of its disabled prisoners first." Among those reaching freedom and the federal line at Vicksburg was Thomas W. Horan, a private in Company H, 65th Indiana Infantry, who had been a prisoner of war for fourteen months. The emaciated Hoosier weighted 106 pounds, having lost "nearly 70 pounds" since his capture. Sadly, Horan endured the horrors of captivity only to die in the *Sultana* explosion a month later. Marvel, *Andersonville*, 234.

57. Sergeant Ely estimated that 100 "carpenters, woodchoppers, etc" accepted the work parole. See Ely Diary, Mar. 19, 1865.

[March 22] It turned quite cool during the night and today is cool and windy. No train came yet for more prisoners for exchange. The men are getting very despondent about getting out.

[March 23] It is very cool and windy today. I went to the creek and took a good bath to day. No sign of any men leaving yet. We moved into our barracks today. We have a good place and are fixed up pretty comfortable.

[March 24] Is quite cold this morning, I went out to get boughs to sleep on. Captain Wirtz came in this morning and said we were all going through to Vicksburg as fast as they could get transportation for us. He also said he never authorized anyone to sell chances for going out in the first squad.[58] And that he did not approve of that way of doing and wanted every thing of the kind to be reported to him.[59]

[March 25] Was quite cool this morning. Rations were late in coming in to day. They were offering chances today for three dollars in green backs. They took out some today, make a break in the Second Division. It is just six months today since I was taken prisoner.

58. According to Ely, the camp sutler was selling chances for early release on March 22 at a price "from 15 to 30 dollars Confederate." On March 24, Ely's company purchased a chance for "eighty dollars greenback, 80 confed and my watch valued at 60 dollars." Ely left Andersonville that afternoon and arrived at the parole camp in Vicksburg, Mississippi, on March 31. Sadly, Ely was one of the more than 1,500 former prisoners who died in the *Sultana* explosion on April 27, 1865. Ely Diary, Mar. 22, 24, 31, 1865.

59. Regardless of Wirz's directive, Pvt. M. J. Umsted described in detail the prisoners' frenzied attempts to buy their release. To go out in the first squad, Umsted claimed that chances were purchased "first for $50.00 but before night it fell to $5.00." Once the first prisoners departed and the prospect for additional releases seemed imminent, "a great many are buying their chances out . . . some for $10.00 some for $5.00 some for $1.00 in greenbacks. So us poor fellows who are destitute of money will be left." The next day Umsted stated that "a great many are buying their chances out this morning for a gold ring or almost any little trinket." His last diary entry was April 2, 1865; at that time he was still a prisoner at Andersonville. Umsted Diary, Mar. 23–26, 1865.

[March 26] This is the Sabbath day again. They took out about two hundred and fifty and all the paroled men outside. News went out of the prison only those who bought out. This is a beautiful day. Cool but very pleasant. We will not likely get out for several days yet.

[March 27] Still cool and pleasant. More moneyed men went out to day. They have got nearly all out who are able to pay to get out. Lots this evening [illegible] the last [illegible] they took out back in again. As no train came for them. The train is reported off the track.[60]

[March 28] Last night it rained nearly all night and until almost noon to day. I went out after wood this morning. The men who went out yesterday are still here. No train yet but numerous reports as to the cause of its delay.

[March 29] It has been raining off and on all day. Then came up a hard thunder storm late in the evening. No further news today in regard to the exchange.

[March 30] It rained very hard during the night. But has cleared off this morning and has been very windy all day. Col. Gibbs came in this evening and said we would go by way of Jacksonville, Florida as soon as transportation could be procured.[61] Gen. [James] Wilson has made a raid on the Vicksburg road and captured Selma and thus stopped the exchange in that direction.[62]

60. According to Umsted, the derailed train caused the death of "a number of Yanks and 6 confederate soldiers." Umsted Diary, Mar. 27, 1865.
61. In February 1865, Gen. Gideon Pillow replaced Gen. John Winder as commissary general of prisoners. In order to expedite the prisoner exchange, which had been greatly hampered by Sherman's cutting off the railroad connections to Savannah, Pillow contacted Gen. Eliakim Scammon, the federal commander at Jacksonville, Florida. The two were acquaintances from their days in the Mexican War, and Scammon, without authorization from the federal government, agreed to accept the released prisoners. Nathaniel Cheairs Hughes Jr. and Roy P. Stonesifer Jr., *Pillow: The Life and Wars of Gideon Pillow* (Chapel Hill: Univ. of North Carolina Press, 1993), 296–98.
62. In the spring of 1865, "Wilson overwhelmed Nathan Bedford Forrest at Selma, Alabama, dispersing the latter's forces, and then Wilson turned east, sweeping

[March 31] Was cloudy and very windy this morning. But during the day cleared off. Report says one of our officers is here on business in connection with the exchange. The truth of this report I cannot vouch for. The time seems *very very* long to us since they stopped taking men out. The difficulty seems to be in getting transportation. God speed the day when we shall once more see the stars and stripes waving on us and feel that their protecting power is over us.

[April 1] Is very pleasant. Report that Captain Wirtz has gone to Macon to get transportation to take us away from here. I am very unwell & have been for some two days past.

[April 2] This is the Sabbath day again, is very warm and pleasant. Captain Wirtz returned today and came in the prison and told us eleven hundred would leave Tuesday and as many Wednesday to go by the way of Jacksonville, Florida.

[April 3] We were called out this morning and taken to Captain Wirtz head quarters to be parolled. As soon as we got there the guards were sent back and we were at liberty to run around. Oh! how our hearts bounded with delight to know and feel that we were once more out from under guard. It was late in the evening before they got through parolling us. We were then sent back into the prison to await the morrow. Oh! how anxiously did we look forward to the morrow.

[April 4] Today we were called out and had four days rations issued us. We were then put on the train and went as far as Albany.[63] When

---

through the remnant of the Confederacy and whirling away its defenders in the greatest independent cavalry movement of the Civil War." See Ezra J. Warner, *Generals in Blue: Lives of the Union Commanders* (Baton Rouge: Louisiana State Univ. Press, 1964), 567. For a full account of the Selma raid, see James Pickett Jones, *Yankee Blitzkrieg: Wilson's Raid Through Alabama and Georgia* (Athens: Univ. of Georgia Press, 1976), 43–66.

63. Between April 4 and 6, Captain Wirz sent 3,425 men to Albany, which left only fifteen prisoners at Andersonville, all of whom were in the hospital. Marvel, *Andersonville*, 236.

we got off and marched out on the Thomasville road four miles to the Blue Springs where we went into camp. No sooner had we gone into camp then Jonnie Reb and Yankee one and all were in bathing. The Blue Springs covers about half an acre in extent. The water is very clear and cold boiling up continually. It is said to have been sounded to the depth of one hundred and fifty feet and no bottom found at that distance. Thus making a splendid place to bathe.

[April 5] We started this morning by sun rise on our road to *Liberty*. Marched with good heart and willing feet. The road was very swampy. We marched about seventeen miles and camped in a dense pine forest. After stopping for awhile we were so sore and stiffened up we could hardly walk. My feet which were blistered from marching barefoot over the rough roads was very painful.

[April 6] We left camp this morning by sun rise. Marched steady all day making about twenty miles to day. We are now within fourteen miles of Thomasville. It is very pleasant marching as it is quite cool. Found it very difficult marching on account of my feet. The road was rough and stony and every step bruising and cutting my feet. Yet I bore it willingly for Liberty was dawning in a distance. And although the blood flowed from wounded feet at every step yet this with Liberty in view was by far preferable to the loathsome prison.

[April 7] Left camp again at sunrise and marched to Thomasville reaching there by four o'clock p.m. We then went into camp to wait further orders. It is with the greatest difficulty I can walk at all today and my feet are very painful.

[April 8] It rained very hard during the night giving us a complete drenching and making the night a miserable one indeed to us. Drew hard tack this morning. While we were waiting for our rations a pale distinguished lady passed by the road side where I sat and said she *"Poor soldier I pity you."* It was the first time I had felt like shedding tears since my capture. But the joy of knowing and feeling that one at least in this wide world would have some sympathy for me. And that to where I least expected to find sympathy almost overpowered me for the time being. And well did I need sympathy for soon after we were ordered back to Andersonville.[64]

[April 9] With sad and heavy hearts we started to retrace our steps; every hope dying with us. Until now I have kept in pretty good heart. But now owing to the state of my health all hope has banished and I feel as (Hyatt expressed it) *They have left us here to die.* Aliens, uncared for and unwept. This the state of my feelings, God grant that it may prove otherwise. We marched back to the camp where we camped the night previous to our arrival at Thomasville.

[April 10] Started early this morning and marched steady all day making about 18teen miles. My feet are very painful indeed.

[April 11] This is my birthday. Oh! What a sorry day it is to me my feet blistered and worn out and having to march barefoot over rough roads. We marched hard all day and camped at night about eight miles from Albany.

[April 12] We marched to within one mile of town where we lay until near night. Where we were marched to the depot where we drew rations. Ready to leave on the train early in the morning.

[April 13] Got on board the train at five o'clock this morning and at nine reached Andersonville where we were again lodged in the prison. Capt. Wirtz told us we would leave again in six days.

[April 14] We drew rations early this morning. We are back in this miserable hole again. I drew the same miserable pittance of meal,

---

64. The reversal occurred because federal department commanders could not agree on the location for exchange; one preferred Savannah, another Jacksonville. Ibid., 236–37.

beans, molasses, salt, and corned beef. All hope has banished, and we are not living but only drawing out a miserable existence. And *death* seems to be the only words of relief for us from our misery and sufferings.

[April 15] Drew rations early. Drew some soap today then went to the creek and had a good bath. It is very windy. I have been very unwell ever since my return. Unless god in his kind providence sees fit to send some mode of relief my time on earth is short for in the state my health is in and the mode of our treatment I cannot stand it much longer.

[April 16] Sabbath morning. It rained very hard last night. I am very unwell. My feet are very painful and sore so it is very difficult for me to walk. We drew rations early this morning. Had preaching in camp by one of the prisoners [and] had a very interesting meeting.

[April 17] It is very warm and sultry today. We drew rations early. Late in the evening we were all ordered to pack up and be ready to leave. And just as the sun was sinking in the west we were marched out of the prison, and taken to the depot and put on the train bound for Macon.

[April 18] Traveled all night crowded one hundred in each car. So we had not even room to sit down. We reached Macon just at day break. And were ordered back to Albany.[65] Capt. Wirtz says he is going to take us back to Thomasville and if our men wont receive us he will parole us and turn us loose. We reached Albany by four o'clock this evening and were marched about one mile from town where we camped on the banks of the Flint River.

65. Originally, the Confederates intended to send prisoners to Savannah via Macon, Georgia. However, Union cavalryman Gen. James H. Wilson moved toward Macon forcing the retreat south to Albany. Interestingly, Adair did not mention a layover at Andersonville when the train stopped for water. Ibid., 237.

[April 19] Lay all day in camp and had a good time bathing in the river. We drew four days rations of hard tack and bacon for going through to Thomasville.

[April 20] We started early this morning and marched hard all day making about twenty miles. My feet are about give out could hardly make camp. But the hope of Liberty urged me on to renewed efforts.

[April 21] Started early again this morning marched steady all day making only about fifteen miles.

[April 22] Started early again this morning. It commenced raining about noon and rained steady all evening. We reached the railroad east of Thomasville late in the evening and went into camp. The rebels told us we would leave on the train at eleven o'clock to night.

[April 23] We got on the train about eleven o'clock last night and reached station No. 12 on the Savannah, Albany and Gulf road about noon. We here took the Florida Central which forms a junction here with the S.A. and G. road and we were soon in the state of Florida.

[April 24] We lay in the train all night and drew rations just before day. We then went on five miles south of Lake City where we got off the train and went into camp in a dense pine forest.

[April 25] Today we were taken out and paroled again. It is just seven months today since I was taken prisoner.

[April 26] They have been paroling all day have just finished paroling the whole camp which numbers three thousand five hundred prisoners.

[April 27] There were numerous reports in circulation to day. One is that we are going to be sent back to Andersonville. But the Rebel

Quarter Master says we go to Baldwin tomorrow to be turned over to our own troops. Oh! that this may prove true that we are so near the boon we seek Liberty. Oh! this *goddess* of *Liberty* would that we might always bask under thy protecting shield.

[April 28] We left camp early this morning on the train for Baldwin. Reaching there mid twelve o'clock. We got off the train and waited until the second train load came up which was then one p.m. As soon as we got off the train one of our majors who was also a prisoner steped out and gave the command (*Fall in*). The joyful hurrah that went up from the prisoners made the surrounding forrest ring. There was a good rush for the railroad. We took right down the railroad from Baldwin leading to Jacksonville. One company of guards going with us to what was called the white house which was halfway between the Rebel and Union lines. There we halted and our Officers and the rebel officers held a consultation for a few minutes when our major again gave the command forward. And we bid adieu to the rebel guards and rebel ones with joyful hearts and bright hopes for the future. On! On! We rushed each seaming desirous of being the first to reach our lines. No stop! No halt except some poor fellow who was completely worn out and could go no farther. At least those of us who were able to stand the trip came in sight of the federal pickets. Oh! with what unutterable joy did we behold the black and glistening faces of the 134th USCI. We felt that those were our friends. And well did they prove themselves to be our friends by their kindness to us in providing for our many wants. And on until the wee hours of the night did they labor in providing food for our frail and exhausted bodies.[66] And it was from them I got my first cup of coffee since the day of my capture.

[April 28, cont'd.] It would be useless to attempt to describe the feelings with which I again behold the stars and stripes again waving

66. Pvt. John Duff agreed with Adair about the reception provided by the black soldiers: "The black troops done us justice. They put us up tents, gave us grub, coffee and every other kindness. We feel better now." Duff Diary, Apr. 28, 1865.

over us and felt that we were surrounded by friends indeed. We lay at Jacksonville until the 10th of May, and drew clothing. The morning of the 10th we left on the steamer *W. W. Coit* going down the St. John's River. We soon sailed out upon the ocean. We kept around the coast to Fernandina where the transport *Cassandra* was waiting for us to convey us to Annapolis, Md. We had a very pleasant voyage only going into port at Hilton Head, SC. And reached Annapolis on the evening of the 14th of May. We lay at camp parole here until the 28th of June when we were discharged and started home. So ended my prison life and so the soldier life; Farwell Prison Farwell Camp. *I am homeward bound.* Have been endearing that word after four years absence. Truly can I appreciate the words (There's no place like home).

Completed Nov 18th 1866 Lyle G. Adair

CHAPTER 7

The Anatomy of a Captivity Narrative

"THE MEMOIR OF A PRISONER can scarcely be set down as a continuous narrative corresponding to the dreary procession of each hour, each day, or even each month," wrote French novelist and former prisoner of war Pierre Boulle. "To follow this procedure would amount to imposing on the reader a boredom as unbearable as that suffered by the captive himself." In this vein, prisoner narratives are best understood "as a series of patterned events" that depend less on chronological time and rely more on a distinct sequence of event scenarios.[1] Boulle's perspective serves as the theoretical basis for *Voices from Captivity: Interpreting the American POW Narrative*, in which author Robert C. Doyle identifies seven captivity narrative event scenarios: precapture, capture, removal, landscape, resistance, release, and lament. These categories of analysis provide the "thematic, dramatic, and interpretive elements needed to describe, explain, clarify, and evaluate the captivity experience."[2] Doyle's event scenarios model serves as the basis for interpreting the prisoner narrative of Sgt. Lyle G. Adair, 111th USCI.

1. Although more well-known for writing *The Bridge over the River Kwai* and *The Planet of the Apes*, Pierre Boulle was a secret agent with the French Resistance during World War II and spent two years as a prisoner of war in French Indochina, from October 1942 until his escape in November 1944. See Pierre Boulle, *My Own River Kwai*, trans. Xan Fielding (New York: Vanguard Press, 1967), 170.
2. Doyle, *Voices from Captivity*, 85.

The precapture autobiography represents the first of the seven event scenarios that comprise the prisoner narrative. As such, a prisoner may explain the motivation of his initial enlistment as well as his notions of duty and honor or "the cause." Sometimes the precapture autobiography includes "idyllic memories of home, family, happiness, freedom, and normalcy."[3] However, the first reference in the Adair diary was September 23, 1864, two days before his capture, and only opaque entries to his precapture life appear in the diary. Anniversaries frequently prompted Adair to reflect on his prewar life. For example, on January 30, 1865, the sergeant noted that "it is just one year to day since I was last mustered into service for three years." Although the commemoration was one of three items Adair recorded in his diary on that day, he did not specify that this tour of duty was his second three-year enlistment. On March 17 he marked the eleventh anniversary of his father's death, and on April 11 he celebrated his twenty-second birthday. Occasionally, Adair mentioned an encounter with a member of his "old co," but more often he identified individuals by name and did not link them to his former unit. Also, just two weeks after his capture, the former private of the 81st Ohio passed through Iuka and Corinth, Mississippi, places where his former unit had fought with distinction. Yet, while in Corinth he only observed that the building he was confined in "was formerly used as post commissary when the Union troops were stationed here." The lack of attention to and reflection on his precapture life clearly demonstrates that Adair wished to have his wartime service defined by his prisoner experience.

Capture, the second of the event scenarios, is marked by a precise and relatively brief moment in actual time. Nevertheless, explanations of capture often comprise a well-articulated, fully developed, and sometimes lengthy portion of the prisoner narrative. According to Doyle, "Universally, soldiers are taught that the objective of war and individual combat is to win. Surrender implies losing, and

3. Ibid.

Americans in particular dislike losers regardless of the context."[4] In the specific case of the American Civil War, surrender was often accompanied by charges of cowardice and dishonor. In fact, a number of Union leaders, both civilian and military, believed that some soldiers allowed themselves to be captured and then paroled in order to avoid the risks of combat.[5]

Such suspicions appeared in the correspondence between Governor David Tod of Ohio and Secretary of War Edwin M. Stanton in early September 1862. On August 30, Confederate forces under the command of Gen. Edmund Kirby Smith captured 4,000 Union soldiers at Richmond, Kentucky. Tod believed that if the Union prisoners had not been paroled so quickly, Smith would have been burdened with the responsibility of controlling and caring for a sizeable number of captives, thereby significantly hampering the general's ability to wage war in the Bluegrass State. Tod advised Stanton: "The freedom in giving pardons by our troops in Kentucky is very prejudicial to the service and should be stopped." Stanton replied: "The evil you mention is one of the most dangerous that has appeared in our army and it is difficult to see what remedy can be applied. There is reason to fear that many voluntarily surrender for the sake of getting home." Because of the prisoner and parolee problems at Ohio's Camp Chase, Tod spoke authoritatively on this issue.[6]

Keeping in mind the distrust and suspicion so prevalent in the North, Adair provided very specific details in his capture story. The inclusion of the central elements of Adair's capture story—the surprising and ferocious nature of the Confederate attack, the tragic death of their brave leader, the lack of ammunition, and the overwhelming Confederate advantage (15,000 to 600)—was designed to deflect any allegation that Company B of the 111th USCI had been derelict or cowardly in the execution of their duty.

---

4. Ibid., 115–16.
5. William B. Hesseltine, *Civil War Prisons: A Study in War Psychology* (Columbus: Ohio State Univ. Press, 1930), 74–76.
6. *OR*, ser. II, vol. 4:499.

To be sure, black units had performed admirably and courageously when given an opportunity to face the elephant. Beginning with the "first significant assault by black troops in the war" at Port Hudson, Louisiana, in late May 1863, and including such notable performances as Milliken's Bend, Louisiana, in June 1863, the Battle of Olustee (Florida) in February 1864, and during the Petersburg phase of the 1864 federal campaign in Virginia, African Americans demonstrated their "potential and effectiveness as combat soldiers."[7] However, on occasion and in "isolated instances," black troops "performed poorly and officers and men exhibited cowardice." For example, nearly three out of ten black soldiers in a company of the 59th USCI jettisoned their rifles during a retreat at the Battle of Germantown (Mississippi) in June 1864. One of the most egregious cases involving black units occurred during the same Forrest raid through northern Alabama that netted Adair and members of the 111th USCI in September 1864.[8]

On September 23, Col. Wallace Campbell, 110th USCI, reported from Athens, Alabama, that the "enemy were tearing up [railroad] track two miles south of him, and that he should move down and drive them away." Late in the afternoon, Campbell and his men arrived by train in the vicinity of Decatur and encountered Confederate troops under the direct command of Col. Jesse Forrest, brother of Gen. Nathan Bedford Forrest. Campbell "deployed skirmishers, . . . drove" the rebels from the track, and extinguished a fire that was burning on a small trestle. Campbell then realized that the enemy had amassed at his rear. He "immediately ordered the train back to town and drove [the rebels] from the track." As he "reached the outskirts of town," Campbell "was attacked by [the] enemy," which he estimated as "some 1,000 strong." He "engaged the enemy for one hour and fifteen minutes, losing 3 men killed and 4 wounded."

7. John David Smith, ed., *Black Soldiers in Blue: African American Troops in the Civil War Era* (Chapel Hill: Univ. of North Carolina Press, 2002), xv–xvii.

8. Glatthaar, *Forged in Battle*, 153.

When he discovered that he could not drive the Confederates from town, Campbell "fell back to the fort at Athens."[9]

Late in the evening of September 23, Campbell learned that General Forrest had a force "estimated at from 10,000 to 12,000, with nine pieces of artillery." Under the cover of darkness, Campbell dispatched two couriers to Gen. John C. Starkweather, commander of the federal post at Pulaski, Tennessee. Nightfall had limited Campbell's options, but he attempted to apprise his commanding officers of his situation. Darkness, however, did not conceal the two couriers dispatched by Campbell: one was shot and killed "on the outside of town," and the other returned to the fort after suffering a shoulder wound. "During the night," Campbell subsequently reported, the troops were "occasionally annoyed by sharpshooters firing" and the sounds of enemy "artillery being brought into position." As daylight unfolded on September 24, Forrest opened fire on the fort "with artillery from three different sides, casting almost every shell inside the works." Campbell rejoined with his 12-pound howitzers but "could not reach" the enemy's lines. At 8:00 A.M., Forrest demanded "an immediate and unconditional surrender of the entire force . . . and property at this post." He promised that "all white soldiers shall be treated as prisoners of war and the negroes returned to their masters."[10]

Colonel Campbell did not participate in the first round of discussions under the flag of truce, but he was told by his emissary that "General Forrest . . . was determined to take the fort, and if he was compelled to storm it no lives would be spared." Initially, Campbell refused the terms of surrender, at which point Forrest requested a "personal interview." Forrest then proposed that Campbell review his forces and see for himself the insurmountable odds and futility of resistance. Campbell consulted "with the commanders of various detachments in the fort, [and] it was decided that if after reviewing

9. *OR*, ser. I, vol. 39, pt. 1:531, 520, 521.
10. Ibid., 521.

the force of General Forrest I found he had 8,000 to 10,000 troops, it would be worse than murder to attempt to hold the works." At 11:00 A.M., Campbell began his inspection tour. Convinced that Forrest commanded an overwhelming force and that Union reinforcements would not arrive in time to help, Campbell surrendered the fort, 538 men and thirty-three officers, just after midday. Campbell's official account of the surrender suggested that, after conducting a council of war and inspecting the enemy forces, he had the support of his officers and reached a logical conclusion.[11]

Campbell, however, was duped by Forrest. The Mississippian had earned a reputation for bluffing his opponents and would often employ "unorthodox" methods to carry out his deception plans. In this instance, Forrest invited Campbell to view his lines to determine the Confederate strength. But during the review, "Forrest referred to his dismounted men as infantry [which] in the distance, the horse-holders gave the impression of large bodies of cavalry." Forrest also ordered "batteries shifted from place to place, inflating the number of guns the Confederates could claim to have." The plan worked "so well that by the time the review ended, Colonel Campbell" was more than convinced of his need to surrender.[12]

Shortly after the surrender, embarrassment gave way to controversy. On October 17, 1864, thirty-one officers surrendered by Colonel Campbell filed a statement of protest condemning the colonel's decision. Among the signatories was Capt. William H. Scroggs of the 111th USCI, a former member of Lyle G. Adair's Company C, 81st Ohio. According to the complaint, of the "forty-five officers present in the fort at the time of this council," only eight were consulted, and "but two officers voted in favor of a surrender, neither of whom had a command in the fort." Furthermore, the complainants argued that the fort possessed military and material stores that "were thought ample for a siege of ten days." Perhaps the most compelling evidence presented by the band of thirty-one was their testimony regarding

11. Ibid., 522–23.
12. Willis, *A Battle from the Start*, 251–52.

the "disposition" of both the white and black troops: "It was everything that any officer could wish of any set of men." Indeed, the men were anxious to test their mettle against Forrest regardless of the risk, and the report claimed that "officers had to exert all their authority, even to threatening to shoot their own men, to restrain them." When news of the surrender circulated through the fort, the men "could scarcely believe themselves, but with tears demanded that the fight should go on, preferring to die in the fort that they made to being transferred to the tender mercies of General Forrest and his men."[13]

They had good reason for concern, especially given the history of Nathan Bedford Forrest—specifically the Confederate assault he led on Fort Pillow on April 12, 1864. The fort, located on the east bank of the Mississippi River and some forty miles north of Memphis, was held by the 13th Tennessee (Union) Cavalry and the 6th United States Colored Light Artillery. After surrounding the fort, Forrest offered a flag of truce and presented terms of surrender. The Union commander rejected the offer. Forrest, fearing that the fort would be aided by the approaching Union gunboat the *New Era*, ordered an assault on the fort, and "with good position and superior numbers, the Confederates quickly overwhelmed Union forces." What transpired next was sheer chaos. Some Union soldiers scampered down the bluff and dove into the Mississippi River hoping to safely reach the *New Era*. Others laid down their arms as an act of surrender. The Confederates, however, continued to fire and charge with fixed bayonets. When the bloodbath ended, almost 50 percent of the Union troops had been killed.[14]

A closer examination of the carnage revealed that the death rate among African American troops was significantly higher than the death rate among white Union troops, 64 percent to 31 percent. Moreover, there were numerous reports that Confederate soldiers

13. *OR*, ser. I, vol. 39, pt. 1:523–26.
14. Heidler and Heidler, *Encyclopedia of the American Civil War*, 2:746–47.

had purposefully targeted black soldiers. Reports of the atrocity outraged the North. The congressional Committee on the Conduct of the War investigated the matter and in May issued a report condemning the Confederate actions. In the end, Fort Pillow became "a rallying cry for black troops." [15] Although captured black troops faced a more uncertain future, white officers of black units clearly understood the danger associated with surrender. [16]

Without doubt, Adair was concerned about the taint of embarrassment and dishonor deriving from Campbell's actions. His unit had faced the same enemy and by all accounts had performed their duty. Thus, the dominant themes of his capture narrative are bravery and fortitude. Furthermore, Adair was certainly aware of Confederate retribution against white soldiers attached to black units, a fact that became demonstrably clear during his removal to his first prison camp.

Following capture, the next event scenario for the soldier-turned-prisoner is the removal, or forced march. This process of relocation from the place of captivity to a recognized prison facility marks "the prisoner's first truly dangerous encounter with the captor's value system." During the removal, "violence becomes commonplace and even ritualized," and "they begin to accept the fact that they are prisoners and gain a clearer vision of the meaning of captivity."[17] The

15. Ibid., 747–48. There is a fairly extensive body of literature on the Fort Pillow Massacre. For the most recent works, see Albert Castel, "The Fort Pillow Massacre: An Examination of the Evidence," in *Black Flag over Dixie: Racial Atrocities and Reprisals in the Civil War*, ed. Gregory J. W. Urwin (Carbondale: Univ. of Southern Illinois Press, 2004); John Cimprich, *Fort Pillow: A Civil War Massacre and Public Memory* (Baton Rouge: Louisiana State Univ. Press, 2005).

16. The black soldiers captured by Gen. Nathan Bedford Forrest were sent to Mobile, where they were impressed to work on the fortifications and defense of the Alabama port city. In January 1865, the *Mobile Advertiser* listed the names of 575 black prisoners of war from the 106th, 110th, and 111th USCI and invited slaveholders to come claim their property. Dudley Taylor Cornish, *The Sable Arm: Black Troops in the Union Army, 1861–1865* (1966; repr., Lawrence: Univ. Press of Kansas, 1987), 178. For more on the black prisoners in Mobile, see Leon Litwack, *Been in the Storm So Long: The Aftermath of Slavery* (New York: Knopf, 1979), 88.

17. Doyle, *Voices from Captivity*, 86, 140–41.

removal includes additional challenges. For instance, five days after his capture, Adair was separated from his officers. The separation of officers and enlisted men was standard practice during the war, and the men were held in separate facilities. Because of the controversial nature of black military service, the bonds between commissioned and noncommissioned white officers in all-black units had been tempered in the furnaces of social prejudice and forged on the field of battle. Indeed, as historian Joseph Glatthaar writes, "combat was the single most important aspect of soldiering, and . . . senior-ranking officers felt more comfortable relying on soldiers who had demonstrated their ability to stand up in battle." Adair had proven his mettle, first as a volunteer with the 81st Ohio and later as a recruiter and dutiful soldier of the 111th USCI. Adair's diary notations indicate that he experienced intense anxiety regarding his separation from his officers. Moreover, the separation of commissioned officers from their men eliminated a critical command structure, which weakened group cohesion and reduced the ability of prisoners to resist effectively their captors.[18]

The transfer of prisoners from the supervision of front line troops to the authority of the rear guards presented new dilemmas for most prisoners, because "treatment at capture depended on the respect of one combatant for the other and ill treatment rarely began before the prisoners met the rear guard."[19] Adair witnessed the contrast in attitude when he arrived at Gainesville Junction near West Point, Mississippi, toward the end of his first removal. There he noticed a "hatred" between the front line soldiers and those who remained on the home front as guards. On one occasion a member of the home guard boasted that if he had captured a white and black soldier together, then he would not have allowed the white soldier to live. The front line soldier responded to this challenge to his manhood by accusing the home guard of cowardice and of being afraid to face the Yankees on the battlefield.

18. Glatthaar, *Forged in Battle*, 182.
19. Doyle, *Voices from Captivity*, 116.

Lyle G. Adair's first removal or forced march lasted some nineteen days. On the third morning of the removal, Adair ate for the first time since his capture. The rations drawn by the prisoners that day consisted of "flour and a little fresh beef." But, as Adair noted in his diary, the men had no way of cooking the flour. As a soldier, Adair could expect to be issued rations on a somewhat regular and consistent basis, along with the proper cooking utensils. However, as a prisoner he faced uncertainty each and every day, depended on the mercy of his captors for sustenance, and realized that the simple act of cooking rations, if they were available, could be a perplexing and distressing ritual. The difficulties he encountered during these nineteen days and the notations in his diary indicate how the new prisoner was gradually becoming aware of and appreciating the meaning of captivity. During his captivity, Adair endured eight removals that lasted a combined forty-seven days, and each removal added a new dimension to the culture of captivity.

The completion of the removal meant the prisoner had arrived at the assigned prison camp. When the prisoner passed through the gates of a prison camp, he not only entered a new physical place, but he also entered a new event scenario within the captivity experience: the prison landscape. Virtually all prisoner narratives feature some type of physical description of their respective facilities. Sergeant Adair arrived at Cahaba Prison in Alabama around 1:00 P.M. on October 11. He chose not to measure the prison's dimensions in terms of feet and inches but, rather, in terms of population. During his first days there, he recalled that "there was some 2,000 men in this building and when all were standing up it was almost impossible to walk around, they were so much crowded." Limited personal space at Cahaba made individual movement not only difficult but dangerous. As prisoners struggled to find adequate places to claim as their own, they had to be alert to the location of the "deadline." Common in most prison camps North and South, deadlines marked boundaries that prevented prisoners from approaching designated areas within the compound. Adair painted a vivid and complex picture of the deadline system at Cahaba. Prison guards had orders to shoot all violators, and they did so with regularity. More than any other feature of the prison landscape, the deadline testified to the captor's near absolute power over the captive.

Without question, the overpopulated prison landscape presented new challenges to Sergeant Adair. One of those challenges was the acquisition and preparation of food. Doyle states that "there is nothing more common in the captivity narratives from colonial times to Vietnam than prisoners' descriptions of food; it becomes an obsession, not only because food and life are inextricably related, but because the act of eating becomes an event—something to anticipate, something to do."[20] Although the quality of the food did not satisfy Adair, he admitted that at Cahaba a sufficient quantity of rations was issued, even if the preparation of these rations added to the prisoners' misery. On October 15 Adair entered Cahaba's cooking area for the first time, and what he witnessed dismayed him. He saw desperate men attempting to build fires with green wood that produced more smoke than flame. Brought to tears by the success of a few fortunate prisoners who mastered the campfire, Adair called the scene "the very picture of dispair." The travails of cooking day, however, eased a few days later when a number of prisoners were transferred to another prison.

Adair was incarcerated in five different prison camps and therefore encountered a variety of prison landscapes. Discernable patterns as well as evolving perspectives can be detected in his diary entries. In describing his second prison landscape, Adair noted Millen's various physical characteristics. Moreover, the deadline was in a state of deterioration, which added to the danger of the prison landscape because of the possibility of arbitrary enforcement. At Millen, Adair experienced firsthand the feared gauntlet. Historically, the gauntlet functioned as a type of prison initiation ritual whereby the captors formed two lines and armed themselves with sticks, rocks, or assorted

20. Ibid., 170.

weapons and forced the captives to run between the two lines. Adair's gauntlet run at Millen did not involve direct physical abuse but, rather, a form of psychological intimidation. While standing in formation outside the gate for roll call, drenched by the torrential rains, Adair and his fellow prisoners incurred the verbal wrath of the guards because of their association with a black regiment. Adair spent twenty-two days at Millen Prison in November 1864. During that time, he wrote of the importance of constructing adequate shelter and indicated that he received fewer rations at Millen than he had at Cahaba.

A two-day trip from Millen during the third week of November 1864 delivered Adair to the Confederate prison camp at Blackshear in southeast Georgia. One historian has called Blackshear Prison "nothing more than an open camp in an out-of-the-way place, surrounded by a guardline, including some heavy artillery pieces."[21] None of the physical features or dimensions of the camp impressed Adair. Instead, the details of the prison landscape at Blackshear were overshadowed by his constant referral to the prisoner exchange question. Rumors of potential prisoner exchanges circulated at Cahaba as well as at Millen. However, speculation at Blackshear reached much greater heights. Of the six diary entries Adair made during his eleven days at Blackshear, all but one include some discussion of his potential release.

Like Blackshear, the Confederate prison camp at Thomasville, Georgia, was little more than an open field with logs and embankments marking the perimeters and guards monitoring the prisoners' movements. Adair's most pressing concern there appeared to have been constructing adequate shelter. Of the twelve diary entries Adair made during his thirteen-day stay at Thomasville, one-third of them include some discussion about shelter and one-fourth some discussion of acquiring wood for heating fuel. Reoccurring rain showers, cold temperatures, and heavy frost forced Adair to spend two days searching for pine boughs, and after eight days he finally felt that he

21. Speer, *Portals to Hell*, 279.

had constructed adequate shelter. The camp's close proximity to a major southwest Georgia town did, however, offer some unique experiences. The people of Thomasville visited the camp on occasion. The first time several women from the city visited to view the "Yankee vandals," but on another occasion the citizenry expressed a form of sympathy or compassion by presenting the prisoners with soap.

Interestingly, Adair spent nearly half of his entire captivity experience at Andersonville, but he never provided a description of the physical dimensions of the famed prison. Perhaps the novelty of sentry boxes, deadlines, and massive pine hewn logs had faded and no longer dominated the canvas on which Lyle G. Adair painted his prison landscapes. Instead, rations, wood, and weather were the most frequently discussed features of Andersonville. The cold, wind, and rain of the winter months at Andersonville placed a premium on securing a constant supply of wood for heating purposes. One month after his arrival, Adair explained the procedure for gathering wood: "We have to carry all the wood we get from one and a half to two miles on our shoulders and it only comes our regular turns about once in every fourteen days." Based on this explanation of prison policy, Adair would personally have been granted permission to collect wood fewer than eight times during his confinement. However, he mentioned his own collection of wood eighteen times in the ninety-five Andersonville diary entries, meaning that nearly 20 percent of the Andersonville entries included a reference to the collection of wood. Moreover, except for rations and weather, no detail of the prison landscape received more attention in Adair's diary than the ritual of gathering wood. The frequent sojourns to the heavily timbered areas miles outside of the camp reinforced the notion of Andersonville's barren and infertile prison landscape. Rather than a mighty, impenetrable fortress, the Andersonville of the winter of 1864–65 more closely resembled "a mile-wide halo of stump-pimpled swamp and swales."[22]

22. Marvel, *Andersonville*, 213.

Desolation may have also been the most appropriate description of the ritual of eating at Andersonville. Upon arriving on the night of December 23, Adair and his comrades were marched into the prison and rations were issued. Adair griped that his rations "consisted of one pint of burned rice. A heavy supper for men who had fasted all day." Within the first week on two separate occasions he commented, "rations short," "rations very short." The rations, however, appeared to have been issued on a regular basis. At various times prisoners used their culinary talents and bartering skills to improve their eating experiences. Adair explained several times the trades and sales he conducted in order to secure a more sustaining meal. But on February 13 a change in the procedure for distributing rations occurred when the Confederate officials sent the cooks into the prison. From that point on, Adair made fewer and less specific comments on rations.

Without question the most dominant feature of the Andersonville Prison landscape was the climate, or weather. Nearly three out of every four of Adair's diary entries contained a reference to the weather. February, the only month that had an entry for every single day, captures Adair's obsession with the weather. Of the twenty-eight entries that month, Adair mentioned the weather on twenty-three different days, slightly more than eight out of ten entries. Occasionally, he commented on a "bright & beautiful day," such as "the Sabbath day" of February 12, or the "warm & pleasant" day of February 19. More often, however, he spoke of the hardship caused by frequent rains and low temperatures. The cold claimed the lives of several prisoners.

As an event scenario, the prison landscape outlined the particular challenges that prisoners of war faced at their respective camps. Each camp Adair entered shared certain common characteristics, but each also presented unique obstacles. On one level, overcoming the prison landscape depended on the prisoner's success in the daily struggle of securing food and shelter from the elements. This primordial contest, though, represented just one aspect of survival or resistance. In fact, survival and resistance mark a distinct event scenario, or category of experience, that includes the prisoner's psychological adaptation to captivity as well as their means for coping with and responding to their confinement.

Doyle's "three distinct choices" made by prisoners of war in the throes of captivity include "active or hard resistance [where] anything that hints at cooperation or collaboration will be rejected; passive resistance, when prisoners either shun their captors or decide to deceive them into mistakenly thinking they are cooperating; and avoidance, when prisoners attempt to dodge a captor's attentive focus."[23] Lyle Adair fell somewhere between passive resistance and avoidance.

On only five occasions during his entire seven months of captivity did Adair even mention the topic of escape by prison inmates. The first occurred less than two weeks after his capture. During his removal to the Cahaba prison, Adair and one of his comrades planned to use the cover of darkness to make an escape from the moving train cars. However, the night layover in Iuka, Mississippi, convinced Adair that his plan could not be successfully executed. Interestingly, four of the five diary entries that Adair recorded on the topic of escapes were made during removals, which typically presented the most opportune time for escape due to lax security practices. Of the five notations on escapes, Adair referenced himself as part of an actual escape plot only once. Thus, it seems reasonable to conclude that Adair personally rejected escape as an expression of hard resistance.

To be sure, the likelihood of a successful escape was minimal. Nevertheless, Union prisoners executed several large-scale breakouts from Confederate prisons. For example, an estimated 500–600 men escaped from Salisbury Prison in North Carolina by simply propping a ladder against a wall and fleeing under the cover of darkness. Perhaps the most famous of the urban escapes occurred at Richmond's Libby Prison in February 1864. Over the course of

23. Doyle, *Voices from Captivity*, 171.

several weeks, prisoners, using clam shells and knives, dug a tunnel that "was eight to nine feet below the surface of the ground, and upon completion, measured sixteen inches in diameter and fifty to sixty feet long." On the night of February 9, a few more than 100 prisoners burrowed out through what "became known as the Great Yankee Tunnel." Search parties discovered two drowned prisoners in the nearby James River and eventually captured forty-eight men; fifty-nine others successfully reached Union lines.[24]

Despite these victories, the number of successful escapes—one where the prisoner actually reached a friendly line—was small, and one need look no further than the Confederacy's most populated prison camp, Andersonville, for proof of the difficulty of the flight to freedom. The prison's morning reports indicate that a total of 328 men escaped from the south Georgia prison, but, as historian Robert S. Davis discovered, "considering that, with some 40,000 different inmates, Andersonville's escape rate comes to only 8 per 1,000 men." Moreover, a closer examination of the records reveals that Andersonville recovered 181 escapees, and that of the remaining 147, more than 100 were recaptured and assigned to new prison camps. Davis concludes that "no more than two dozen men" escaped from Andersonville and reached Union lines. He pointed to the prison's isolated location, the poor health of the prisoners, and a suspicious and retributive Southern civilian population as contributing to the lack of successful escapes.[25]

Certainly, these factors influenced Adair's decision-making process. In addition, unsuccessful escapes bore dire consequences. Escapees often suffered serious wounds from Confederate recovery dogs that were sometimes used in the capture of runaway prisoners, and they also risked being shot by trigger-happy guards. On the morning of December 6, 1864, Adair witnessed firsthand the dangers of foiled escapes when two of his mess mates attempted to

24. Speer, *Portals to Hell*, 222, 232–33.
25. Robert S. Davis, "Escape from Andersonville: A Study in Isolation and Imprisonment," *Journal of Military History* 67 (Oct. 2003): 1072–73, 1067.

escape. Shortly thereafter, the Confederate authorities recaptured both prisoners; one of the prisoners was shot in the hip by a guard. Aside from the high risks and the diminished prospects for a successful escape, Adair spurned the notion of escape because he was absolutely convinced that an exchange was imminent. Whether the source was the Confederate captors, newspapers, or newly arriving prisoners, rumors of an exchange or parole flowed freely through all of Adair's camps of confinement. Consequently, he filled his diary with thoughts of freedom. In fact, slightly more than one-third of the ninety-five total diary entries from Andersonville contained some reference to an exchange, making his release the second-most-discussed topic in the diary, even more than rations.

Although he effectively avoided hard resistance, Adair did not embrace assimilation, "an active process undertaken by prisoners by their own free will."[26] The motives of assimilators were varied. Some expressed a genuine fear that imprisonment equaled a death sentence and sought any alternative to confinement. In some instances, prisoners assimilated as part of an authentic embrace of the captor's cause and culture, while others held to the utilitarian incentive of being able to leave a camp for a different environment. For whatever reason, some Union captives took unusual steps to relieve their despair and agreed to serve the Confederacy in some capacity. These men became known as Galvanized Rebels or Oath Men. The number of Union prisoners who accepted the Confederate offer startled many Union inmates. Sergeant Adair estimated that on January 27, 1865, around 300 Union captives left the Andersonville prison. A month later one of his mess mates, Alex McWhorter, joined the Confederacy. Adair understood why his fellow prisoners made their decisions to become Galvanized Rebels. Still, he viewed them with hatred and condemnation, which he clearly expressed after his first encounter with one at Millen in early November 1864: "They volunteer and take an oath to support and defend the enemies of

26. Doyle, *Voices from Captivity*, 195.

their father country. And thus forgive themselves and disgrace their friends and relations and the name of soldier. For they cannot be true soldiers and thus prove false to their colors."

On occasion, Adair practiced passive resistance. At Blackshear, Adair mentions for the first time the practice of flanking for rations, whereby prisoners would move around to different groups when rations were being dispensed in order to receive extra portions. They were quite successful at Blackshear. In fact, Adair recorded that the Confederate quartermaster believed that he had issued in excess of 600 extra rations, which may explain why Adair did not receive any rations two days later. Also, Adair's division rejected a Confederate offer to move into some recently constructed barracks at Andersonville. He offered no explanation for the decision. Perhaps, the camaraderie and self-reliance within the tents or she bangs convinced Adair to forego the improved living conditions in the barracks. Most passive resisters utilized deception as their instrument of resistance. For Adair, ration flanking, the refusal to accept barrack-style housing, and purchasing, trading, and selling rations in violation of camp rules all constituted forms of passive resistance. His diary entries revealed virtually no personal interaction with any guards or prison officials; he avoided contact and thereby confrontation. Ultimately, "effective resistance is not related so much to heroism as to a pattern of behavior based on a commitment to community values."[27]

For Adair, those values rested on a deep-seated faith and trust in the righteousness of the Union cause. He began the diary with the capture story and carefully chronicled the heroic struggle of Company B in patriotic tones. Just prior to his removal from Cahaba, Adair received word from his former officers who were held on parole at Enterprise, Mississippi. He learned that they were residing in private houses in town and enjoyed many comforts not available to most prisoners. The contrast astonished him. Still, he persevered.

27. Ibid., 194.

"Why complain," he remarked. "We are in for it, let us bear it like true soldiers who are suffering for the cause of our beloved country which we have espoused." At Millen, Adair once again expressed his unwavering support for the Union cause. This time, on November 8 during a mock presidential election, he cast his ballot for Abraham Lincoln and boasted that a strong majority supported the president. As rumors circulated about possible peace talks in late January 1865, Adair naturally yearned for freedom but confessed that if peace were brokered, he desired an "honorable peace"; otherwise, he preferred to remain in prison rather than have "any thing done for our release which will bring disgrace upon the union arms." Despite some moments of despair, even as late as March 31, 1865, he remained faithful to the Union cause and repledged his allegiance. The depth of his patriotism and fervent nationalism was a sustaining force during his captivity.

The final event scenarios—release and lament—consist of an explanation of the logistical as well as emotional processes associated with the return to freedom. Historically, prisoners gained their freedom "in one of four ways: escape or self-liberation; rescue by raiders who enter hostile battle zones and withdraw captured soldiers; liberation by a large military operation against a POW camp during hostilities; or by release by an agreement or contract including cartel-exchange . . . or treaty of peace."[28] In the case of Adair, he returned to the Union lines as part of a wholesale exchange at the war's end. The diary entries for this ten-day odyssey were often brief, primarily covering the prisoners' location, route of travel, living conditions, and the availability of supplies. On two separate occasions, on April 20 and 27, Adair revealed the emotional dimensions of this final removal. He reclaimed his lost freedom on April 28, and his description constituted the single longest daily entry in the diary. The key passage of the April 28 entry entailed a confession offered by Adair on behalf of his fellow prisoners: "It

28. Ibid., 231.

would be useless to attempt to describe the feelings with which I again behold the stars and stripes again waving over us and felt that we were surrounded by friends indeed."

Apparently, Adair cared as little for the release and lament dimensions of the event scenarios as he did the precapture phase. Indeed, he remained in Jacksonville, Florida, until May 10, at which time he departed for Annapolis, Maryland, where he remained in the federal parole camp for six weeks. And yet he did not record a single detail of this experience other than specific locations and means of transportation. He concluded the diary by simply stating: "So ended my prison life and so the soldier life; Farwell Prison Farwell Camp. *I am homeward bound.* Have been endearing that word after four years absence. Truly can I appreciate the words (There's no place like home)."

Robert Doyle's event scenario model provides an important starting point for understanding the Civil War prisoner experience. In the case of Lyle G. Adair, the eight removals or forced marches prior to release constitute one of the most dominant themes in the diary. Although imposing physical challenges was part of the removal, the uncertainty that accompanied relocation—which for Adair was on average once every nineteen days—was certainly a traumatizing aspect of captivity. The five prison landscapes shared some common characteristics, and the frequency with which Adair discussed wood and the weather emphasized the primordial struggle faced by most Civil War prisoners. Survival also depended on some type of mental adaptation, and for Adair an unwavering faith in the Union cause helped sustain him.

Suggested Reading

AN EXCELLENT INTRODUCTION to the study of Civil War prison camps and the prisoner of war experience is Lonnie Speer's *Portals to Hell: Military Prisons of the Civil War* (Mechanicsburg, Pa.: Stackpole Books, 1997). In addition to providing profiles of both Northern and Southern camps, Speer covers such topics as African American prisoners of war, disease, death rates, escapes, attitudes and actions of guards, and rations. Also, William Hesseltine's edited *Civil War Prisons* (Kent, Ohio: Kent State University Press, 1962) covers several camps, including Andersonville, Fort Warren, Rock Island, Elmira, Libby, and Johnson's Island, and tells the stories of two Union officers who were prisoners of war. Destined to be the authoritative work on Civil War prison policy is Charles W. Sanders Jr.'s *While in the Hands of the Enemy: Military Prisons of the Civil War* (Baton Rouge: Louisiana State University Press, 2005). With meticulous detail, Sanders explains how military and civilian decision makers "deliberately and systematically" implemented policies that led to the mistreatment and unnecessary deaths of tens of thousands of Confederate and Union prisoners. A reliable and time-tested complement to *While in the Hands of the Enemy* is William Hesseltine's *Civil War Prisons: A Study in War Psychology* (Columbus: Ohio State University Press, 1930), which covers primarily the exchange issue; the prisons, North and South, with an emphasis on Libby and Andersonville; and the Northern war psychosis generated by reports of mistreated Union prisoners. For Civil War prison policies in a historical context see Paul J. Springer's *America's Captives: Treatment of POWs from the Revolutionary War to the War on Terror* (Lawrence: University Press of Kansas, 2010). James M. Gillispie's *Andersonvilles of the North: The Myths and Realities of Northern Treatment of Civil War Confederate Prisoners* (Denton: University of North Texas Press, 2008) is a serious reexamination of Union prison camp policies and excels in its study of medical issues connected to the captivity experience. Roger Pickenpaugh's *Captives in Gray: The Civil War Prisons of the Union* (Tuscaloosa: University of Alabama Press, 2009) covers similar ground.

There are a host of scholarly treatments of individual Civil War prisons. A partial list would include Michael Gray, *The Business of Captivity: Elmira and Its Civil War Prison* (Kent, Ohio: Kent State University Press, 2001); Roger Pickenpaugh, *Camp Chase and the Evolution of Union Prison Policy* (Tuscaloosa: University of Alabama Press, 2007); Benton McAdams, *Rebels and Rock Island: The Story of a Civil War Prison* (DeKalb: Northern Illinois University Press, 2000); Alan Huffman, *Sultana: Surviving Civil War, Prison, and the Worst Maritime Disaster in American History* (New York: Harper Collins, 2009); William O. Bryant, *Cahaba Prison and the Sultana Disaster* (Tuscaloosa: University of Alabama Press, 1990); William Marvell, *Andersonville: The Last Depot* (Chapel Hill: University of North Carolina Press, 1994); John W. Lynn, *800 Paces to Hell: Andersonville* (Fredericksburg, Va.: Sergeant Kirklands Museum and Historical Society, 1999); Louis A. Brown, *The Salisbury Prison: A Case Study of Confederate Military Prisons, 1861–1865* (Wilmington, N.C.: Broadfoot, 1992); Brian Temple, *The Union Prison at Fort Delaware: A Perfect Hell on Earth* (Jefferson, N.C.: McFarland Press, 2003).

Some important studies of the captivity experience from the prisoners' perspective include J. Michael Martinez, *Life and Death in Civil War Prisons: The Parallel Torments of Corporal J. Wesley Minnich, C.S.A. and Sergeant Warren Lee Goss, U.S.A* (Nashville: Rutledge Hill Press, 2004); Philip Burnham, *So Far from Dixie:*

Confederates in Yankee Prisons (Landam, Md.: Taylor Trade Books, 2003); Frances Harding Casstevens, *Out of the Mouth of Hell: Civil War Prisons and Escapes* (Jefferson, N.C.: McFarland, 2003).

Recently scholars have addressed the issue of Civil War prisons in history and memory, particularly Benjamin G. Cloyd, *Haunted by Atrocity: Civil War Prisons in American Memory* (Baton Rouge: Louisiana State University Press, 2010); Robert Scott Davis, *Ghosts and Shadows of Andersonville: Essays on the Secret Social Histories of America's Deadliest Prison* (Macon, Ga.: Mercer University Press, 2006); Peter H. Wood, *Near Andersonville: Winslow Homer's Civil War* (Cambridge, Mass.: Harvard University Press, 2010).

Finally, everyone who undertakes the study of the American prisoner-of-war experience should at some point read Robert C. Doyle, *Voices from Captivity: Interpreting the American POW Narrative* (Lawrence: University Press of Kansas, 1994).

Index

Campbell, Wallace, 100–102, 104
Camp Lawton, 35. *See also* Millen
  Prison
Chamberlin, W. H., 2, 3, 8
Cobb, Howell, 34–35
Coffin, Levi, 4
Committee on the Conduct of the
  War, 37n17, 104
Contraband camps, 10–12
Cooper, Samuel, 34–35

Dewey, J. A., 18, 18n4
Dix-Hill Cartel, 63
Dodge, Grenville, 10–11
Duffield, Peter W., 72

81st Ohio Volunteer Infantry: abolitionist views of troops, 4–5; at
  Corinth, 7–8; formation of, 2; part
  of Department of Missouri, 3–4; re-
  enlistment eligibility, 8; at Shiloh, 7
Emancipation Proclamation, 12, 63
Evans, Samuel, 9

Fannin, James, 50
55th USCI, 12
59th USCT, 9
Fink, Sollayman E., 29
First Alabama Infantry of African
  Descent, 12
First Confiscation Act, 5
Forno, Henry, 45, 49, 50
Forrest, Jesse, 100
Forrest, Nathan Bedford, 14, 16, 17,
  100, 101, 102, 103
Fort Pillow Massacre, 103–4
Fremont, John C., 3; proclamation of,
  5–6

Gardner, Amanda, 29n18
Gibbs, George, 86, 89
Gibson, John, 72
Grant, Ulysses S.: view of contraband
  camps, 11, 63

Hafer, William H., 72
Hampton Roads Conference, 79
Hattaway, James, 28
Hawes, Jesse, viii
Hood, John Bell, 73

Johnson, C. R., 34n5
Johnson's Island Prison, 55, 55n31

Lathrop, William H., 16, 17, 18
Lawton, Alexander, 35
Libby Prison, 110
Lightcap, William, 50, 51
Lincoln, Abraham: death of, 24, 63; elec-
  tion of 1864, 41; on Fremont Procla-
  mation, 5; second inauguration, 85.
  See also Emancipation Proclamation
Long, Lessel, 51

Mader, John, 10, 28
McElroy, John, 46
McEwen, Jack, 71, 72
McWorter, Alex, 72, 82
Middleton, Arden, 2
Millen, Georgia, 33
Millen Prison: capacity and size, 36;
  comparisons to Andersonville, 36,
  39n22; disease and death rates, 36;
  first arrivals, 35; Galvanized Rebels,
  40n23, 42; local opposition to,
  34n5; origins, 33–35. *See also* Camp
  Lawton
Miller, Allen, 72
Minnis, J. B., 17
Monroe, Chas, 72
Montgomery, Alabama, 31; prison
  camp at, 31n21

Nelson, Joseph, 10

Oberlin-Wellington Case, 5
111th USCI: formation of, 9–10, 100;
  capture of, 100–105
134th USCI, 95